The Art of Teaching Confirmation

LAURA R. LANGHOFF

www.carpentersministrytoolbox.com OR www.dceministry.blogspot.com

Published 2014 by Carpenter's Ministry Press.

ISBN: 0692247661
ISBN-13: 978-0692247662

DEDICATION

To all the teachers of the Word as they do their most important job.

To God be the glory, great things He has done!

CONTENTS

FOREWORD

What would your next confirmation lesson plan look like, and why? This small book will help you answer those questions and will strengthen your leadership in Christian education.

Laura Langhoff, an experienced Christian educator, has assembled a significant collection of strategies useful in teaching the Christian faith, supported by introductory chapters about the nature of the adolescents likely to be participating in confirmation instruction. She attends to the reality of the faith—not just facts or information, but a living relationship with God in Christ—and to the reality of teaching.

Chapter One opens the door to this work, that adolescents in confirmation are not adults and not simply minds "on a stick" (sorry, this writer lives in Minnesota, where anything can be put on a stick at the State Fair), but whole persons, hormones likely raging, identity developing, in the context in America of a culture that does much to contradict the Christian faith. Chapters Two and Three offer patterns for planning lessons and the curriculum that guides them. Chapters Four through Eight offer an array of options for actual teaching activities, strategies to take you and your students to the goals you wish them to achieve for the day and for the course.

Two significant realities underlie this text: the Gospel of Jesus Christ and the "law" that we need to make informed choices about young people finding their places in that faith, in the Body of Christ. Christian information in confirmation? Surely, but not only that. "Opportunity to develop their own thoughts" (p. 31). Surely, but not only that. "The Bible is about real people with real lives and real problems" (p 32). The Gospel of God's great work in Christ gave those people in their lives, and gives us now in our lives caring for confirmands, the confidence to move forward.

I would love to undo, to challenge an assumption of this text, that confirmation is a practice of the church on behalf of its adolescents, a tradition to be maintained in the 21st century. But the assumption is alive and well among us: this text is a good guide for doing it well. Doubly, Laura proposes not least with references to Luther that we need this practice, that parents are not in a position to teach their children the faith. As soon as I offer the counter proposal, that parents could do it each evening over the dinner table, you would remind me of how few families are together at the dinner table, or together at all. Point well taken. Truth be told, when I realized I had missed family faith conversations with my children, we talked daily for some months during the ten minute commute to school: there was no confirmation alternative. Make good plans for your confirmation instruction. If you are new to serious reflection about how to carry out that instruction, this text will serve you well.

Why would Laura take time to write such a book? Likely for the same reason you would read it: "interesting and meaningful lessons for adolescents with the goal of moving them from factual knowledge and recitation to a deeper understanding and internalization of religious concepts," (p 51). "These are a few of the many ways to help students interact with the Word of God . . . to help students think about their faith in ways that will help them understand it and further share it with the people in their world" (p. 58).

Indeed, to God be the glory as you work with this book, in Jesus' name.

Rev. Dr. Rich Carter, DCE
Professor of Religion and Theology, Emeritus
Concordia University, St. Paul

PREFACE

This book shares the secrets of secondary education with confirmation educators. Maya Angelou said, "Do the best you can until you know better. Then when you know better, do better." Experiencing it as a student does not make us good teachers of confirmation. In light of what we know about how children learn and educational policy and practice it is time now to do better. It is time to take that information and apply it to confirmation. By changing just a few things about how they teach, confirmation educators can bring about a more significant understanding of the Bible and their faith for adolescents and with the help of the Spirit, a more meaningful personal relationship with God and His Son, Jesus Christ. This is not the next great confirmation curriculum and it doesn't talk about all the different aspects of confirmation program models. It is intended to provide insight as to how to help adolescents interact with the information in a more meaningful way at their developmental level. There's an old saying, "If you give a man a fish he will eat for a day but if you teach him to fish he will eat for a lifetime (Ritchie, 1885). This book draws on my background as a professional educator with an M.A. in classroom instruction, years of experience in public secondary education, and a Director of Christian Education certification in the Lutheran Church, in order to teach you how to fish, so you may educate better for a lifetime!

I give thanks to God for the gifts that He has showered upon me and for the courage to share them with the world. I also thank Him for my family, my cousin Dawn Hines, the pastors in the Minnetonka Circuit of the Minnesota South District (LC-MS), and Dr. Rich Carter for their support and encouragement.

Cover art is graciously shared by Camp Omega in Waterville, MN.

INTRODUCTION

This book was born out of two convictions. First, all people, including teenagers, are looking for the truth. They want to know what's real and what life is all about. But while popular psychology tells them to find it within themselves, the more they look inward, the more lost they feel. The ultimate truth is only found in God and the ultimate grace and forgiveness in Jesus Christ. Second, strong faith comes more from knowledge of God (Father, Son, and Spirit) and His promises than it does from feeling "in love" with Jesus. God does not say, "Be still and feel my presence." He says, "Be still and *know* that I am God" (emphasis added, Psalm 46:10). Relying on religious feelings instead of God's promises deceives people into believing that feeling God's presence is more important than knowing He is present. It is possible to correct this and other deceptions through education.

There are a few problems with how we educate in the church. First, we have a tendency to educate for information rather than understanding and application. While knowing the information is necessary, providing opportunities for students to interact with it is what helps them understand it on a deeper level. Second, along with public education, we've fallen into the trap of thinking students need to find Christian education attractive, fun, or entertaining, when instead it needs to be interesting, meaningful, and intellectually challenging, and make no mistake, it can be. This book is an attempt to change that, especially with regard to confirmation.

Over the years, confirmation has been defined differently by many different groups and individuals. Families commonly consider it a culminating rite of passage and observe it with a special celebration. The *Lutheran Service Book* (2006) says "Confirmation is a custom of the church that links the catechumens to their Baptism, celebrates the reception of the Lord's Word among them and, in cases where the candidates have not yet communed, welcomes them to the Lord's Table." It is an important custom within the church; however, the understanding of confirmation's link to Baptism is not fully understood by the young participants. The purpose of confirmation is to support and strengthen a person's sacramental life of faith (Burreson, 2009). It is not to be an ending point in the education of believers, but a beginning as Matthew 28:19 tells us to make disciples of all nations, "teaching them" about God and what Jesus sacrificed for them. Sustaining a *life* of faith requires ongoing training in the Word leading toward faith maturity, making confirmation one of many celebrations in the journey of a *life* of faith that begins with Baptism.

In a society where even in church, how a person feels has become more important than what a person knows, it is more important than ever to make sure that people understand Christianity from its Biblical foundation. Nobody can share what they don't know. The purpose of confirmation is similar to that of education. While students are educated in hope that they become life-long learners, believers are educated in the Word in hope that they become life-long *believers*. All of this reinforces the need for well-trained confirmation teachers.

Looking at popular music, movies, and television shows, it would appear that adolescent youth are not interested in religion. Many are not open about it and won't initiate a conversation about it; however, a study in the *Journal of Adolescent Health* (Holder, et al., 2000) found that more than 85% of youth aged 11 to 25 said they believe in God and more than 90% that religion was at least somewhat important in their lives. This staggering percentage implies that far more adolescents believe in God than one might think and confirms the importance of teaching the truth of the Gospel, as recorded in the Bible, in a meaningful way, so that they are not led astray by inaccurate information provided by friends or popular evangelists.

Friends and social norms in public schools can have a strong influence on choices made by adolescents, as can being educated in their faith and studying the Bible (Barrett, et al., 2007). Religious participation has been found to have a positive effect on the social choices adolescents make specifically with regard to alcohol, drug use, and sex. The National Longitudinal Study on Adolescent Health (Resnick, et al., 1997) found that families who attend church and pray are less likely to have adolescent youth involved in alcohol, drug and marijuana use, and participating in early sexual activity. Everybody needs a moral compass and if one is not provided it will be created based on the beliefs of the society around them. Those who do not know, easily stray to what is popular, fun, and/or entertaining. Families who practice religious beliefs and support Biblical education such as confirmation are helping to provide a moral compass and reinforcing moral behavior in their adolescents.

There comes a time when people have to choose whether or not they will stand for what they believe or cave in to the pressures of a society that believes people can and should make their own rules and create their own moral compass. Having the strength to stand up for what one believes during a time when peer pressure is at its greatest requires the knowledge to support that belief, and if that belief is based on the teachings of the Bible, adolescents need to be solid in that, which begins with a strong confirmation program.

Most confirmation students are middle-school-aged youth who have distinct learning needs due to their developmental stage of life. Confirmation educators may not be aware of those needs, which makes it imperative that they be trained in the effective teaching of that age group. While one can never discount the power of the Word of God in religious education, the quality of teaching may either help or hinder these important teachings. Confirmation educators not only reinforce religious beliefs, but can address inconsistencies adolescents hear from family members (Ozorak, 1989), friends, and their peer group (Regnerus, Smith, & Smith, 2004). Quality teaching includes an understanding of students' physical and emotional development, how learning occurs, how a strong curriculum is developed to achieve specific learning goals and how to create opportunities for deeper understanding. In short, quality teaching takes thought before action and preparation before practice.

The Age Old Question: Parents or Pastors?

One of the greatest ongoing discussions in the church is whether or not parents or pastors should be responsible for the religious education of children. I have an opinion on that along with everyone else, but let me share the opinion of Martin Luther, the reason most people say parents should do this very important job. In a treatise to the councilmen of all cities in Germany, Luther (1525) expressed his desire that Christian education be a civil responsibility. To those who would say that the Christian education of children is a parental responsibility he says, "Very true: but if the parents neglect it, who is to see to it? Shall it on that account remain undone and the children be neglected?" He then shares his reasons why parents should not be the ones to provide Christian education to their children (as taken directly from his 1525 treatise).

- There are those who lack the piety and decency, even if they had the ability, to do it.
- The great majority of parents are, alas! unfitted for this work and do not know how children are to be trained and taught, for they themselves have learned nothing but how to provide for the belly; whereas it takes persons of exceptional ability to teach and train children aright.
- Even if parents were able and willing to do it themselves, they have neither the time nor the opportunity for it, what with their other duties and housework.

Do any of these reasons apply today? Based on this treatise, Luther would prefer the local government provide religious education to children before leaving that task to parents. Prior to a few sections of the Small Catechism (1986), originally written in 1529, Luther uses the phrase, "As the head of the family should teach them in a simple way to his household." Many church leaders take that to mean that Luther believed it was the father's responsibility to teach confirmation to his children. However, later in the preface of that same book Luther clearly states that he found that "the common people, especially in the villages, have no knowledge whatever of Christian doctrine, and, alas! many pastors are altogether incapable and incompetent to teach [so much so, that one is ashamed to speak of it]." He also tells the bishops that they are neglecting their duty in not educating the people and urges them to do so! He continues to say, "If you cannot do more… at least drill the people." In his opinion, barring the ability of the government to publicly educate all children in Christian doctrine, Martin Luther thought it was the job of the clergy, and barring the ability of the clergy, the parents.

Thanks to excellent seminary education, pastors now have strong knowledge of the Bible, church history, and Christian doctrine. Luther said, "If you cannot do more…." Knowing what we do about educating middle school adolescents, we can now do more.

Whether or not a confirmation program is more or less traditional, done through a youth ministry program, includes well-trained parents, has a service component, and/or involves retreats is not as important as it having strong education practices that will increase meaning and understanding, and, with the help of the Holy Spirit, grow faith.

1
DEVELOPMENT:
WHAT'S THE DEAL WITH THESE KIDS?

Many people will think this is the most boring or most unnecessary part of the book. They want to know the ten steps or five strategies that will make their students sit up and be excited to be there, ask intelligent questions, and hang on their every word showing such great interest that they'll rush home to read the Bible and learn their memory work. Unfortunately it's not that easy. Confirmation students are 11 to 14 years old, but probably most will be 12 or 13, which puts them about half way through their brain development. If you've ever known a 13 year old you know their life is all about them, what's happening to them, what's going on with their friends, and how you (or any adult) couldn't possibly understand anything they're going through.

Every good teacher knows who they're teaching. We can't connect with students if we don't know something about them. Who are these kids? What's going on with them physically, socially, and cognitively?

Physical Development

Physically, middle school students experience major body changes as their hormones begin preparing them for sexual activity and fertility. If you don't remember it or haven't witnessed a child go through it, let me remind you that those changes can take up most of their waking thoughts. Hofmann and Greydanus (as cited in American Psychological Association [APA], 2002) and *No Child Left Behind* (2005) list those changes.

- Their sex organs are coming alive.
- There may be rapid skeletal growth that could cause growing pains.

- They are overly aware of their own body changes.
- They are also very aware of how their friends' bodies are changing.
- The physical changes are distracting.
- They start comparing their bodies to that of their same sex friends.
- They start noticing the changes in the opposite sex.
- They begin feeling physical attraction to the opposite sex.
- They begin to have body odor.
- They have hair growing in places they don't want to mention.
- Hormones, hormones, hormones!

While we see normal physical development, our students may not feel normal at all. They may feel they're wearing blinking neon signs every time they notice something different about their bodies or somebody else's and they are aware of how quickly their bodies are changing compared to their peers. They can feel awkward and uncomfortable in their own skin which can affect their self-perception and consume their thoughts.

As hormones begin coursing through their bodies, sex becomes a greater topic of curiosity and discussion. Unfortunately, the first place they go for advice is either their friends or people on the Internet, both of which are happy to share the basic physical act and exciting feelings, but will conveniently forget both the emotional and spiritual aspects of two becoming one. At their young age and limited experience they also don't understand that "having sex" is a progression of behaviors that includes petting and oral sex, making the middle school years a perfect time for meaningful discussion on that topic (APA, 2002).

Nearly 17% of middle schoolers and 49% of high schoolers admit to having sexual intercourse (Resnick et al., 1997). If almost half of our high school students are having sexual intercourse even more are engaged in some form of sexual activity. Why not? The message they get from their friends and society is that sex is another recreational activity that people do all the time with anybody they meet. Given these statistics it's obvious that discussions surrounding sexual activity need to happen earlier than high school. While it can be uncomfortable, it is a good time to start discussing physical relationships and how God created us and gave us the gift of physical intimacy. Tread with care and respect for the feelings and experiences these kids may be having.

The key to a successful discussion regarding sex is to make it a discussion about people in general as opposed to a lecture where they are told what to think or do. Give students a vehicle to ask anonymous questions, and don't be nervous about it. Keeping it simple and telling them "Don't do it!" without giving them real reasons why they shouldn't or allowing them to think about it is a mistake. The more comfortable and open we are the more comfortable and open they will be. It may not be ideal for this discussion to be a confirmation lesson, but it needs to happen at this time and the sixth commandment is definitely an opening and can include what the Bible says about sex, multiple wives, concubines, etc.

Social and Emotional Development

By nature, at this time in their lives, middle school students become very social creatures and parents or all adults somehow become less intelligent and "don't get it." The center of a young adolescent's world shifts from family and parents to peers, who begin to have greater impact on their choices as, socially and emotionally, they are beginning the process of independence. As noted by Obenchain and Taylor (2005) and Santrock (cited in APA, 2002), a number of things are happening during this stage of life.

- Their world grows and moves outside of their family and neighborhood.
- They want to spend more time with peers and less with the family.
- They choose friends and peer groups without parental input.
- They look to peers for support and advice.
- The need to belong to a group becomes *extremely* important.
- They begin searching for their identity as individuals and may even try on different personalities or styles for a week or even a few months.
- They begin to question authority or find fault with adults.
- Friends and the social climate of the school start affecting their beliefs.
- Mainstream and social media have an impact on their beliefs.
- Their friendship relationships become more complicated as they learn what it takes to keep a friend, and how to deal with more complicated social behavior and social cues.

It's Time to Fly

The middle school years are the years these little birds realize they have wings and the high school years are when they start to use them. Parents watch with trepidation as their children pull away from them and they feel they have less influence. What they don't realize is that a child's confidence and feeling of competence is directly linked to feeling emotionally close and accepted by their parents (Ohannessian, Lerner, Lerner, & Eye (as cited in APA, 2002)).

It may also be noticed, much to their parents' dismay, that middle school students begin choosing their own friends and peer groups. They will make some poor choices and experience emotional pain as they build social skills, learning that it takes different skills to make a friend than it does to keep a friend (APA, 2002). The sense of needing to belong to a peer group can become all-consuming to the point where they may make inappropriate choices in order to feel connected. It's during these years that peer pressure takes hold and begins to have a greater influence on their lives. Navigating relationships at this stage can become quite a challenge along with having to decide which friendships to nurture, and what groups, teams or clubs to join.

The World Outside of the Nest

When we think about an elementary child's world, it is pretty small. It includes the family and their elementary classmates, who are usually chosen for them. The family is the center of the child's life socially and emotionally at that time and is where boundaries are set with regard to behavior. Moving up to middle school or junior high school is a big step from this standpoint. They go from a small 30-student classroom to five or six classes and 150 to 180 new "friends" most of whom are different from them. It's through their new peers that students begin broadening their world view (Santrock (as sited in APA, (2002)) as they take their first big step away from the family unit and get a closer view of how others live in and navigate the world. Thankfully, it is a positive family culture that instills the morals and ethics a student brings to the world throughout their elementary years and is the most significant factor when it comes to students choosing behaviors such as smoking, abusing alcohol or drugs, participating in sexual behaviors and waiting to have sexual intercourse (Resnick et al., 1997).

It is also through identification with peers that young adolescents begin to define moral judgment and values. Their peers provide a temporary reference point from which they can begin comparing the morals and values instilled by their parents to the behavior, beliefs, morals, and values of others. While doing this they are secretly looking for ways to identify with their parents (APA, 2002). Though their behavior may often indicate otherwise, while they are testing the morals instilled by the family, at the same time they're hoping and trying to prove them correct. This is a good time for students to have other positive, strong adult relationships as spiritual anchors whether they are with other family members, parents of close friends, pastors, or youth directors (APA, 2002). Confirmation can play a pivotal role in this growth process.

Social Church Life

Wouldn't it be great if students loved learning about God so much that they read the Bible every day and rushed to church just to learn more? Unfortunately, at 12 or 13 years old, most confirmation students are new at learning how to navigate and cope with the world and at this point, relational interests take center stage. Whether or not a student's friendship group attends church (either the same or a different church) has an effect on individual students' religious attendance and their perceptions of the importance of religion (Regnerus et al., 2004). Developing relationships within their confirmation group makes a huge difference as to whether or not they want to attend both classes and church services. In middle school, classmates and the social climate of the school influence the religious beliefs of the adolescent. Not only do they compare morals and values, they begin comparing religious beliefs to that of their increasingly more important peer group as well. This indicates the importance of confirmation beginning at this time in their lives and how it can help solidify their personal Christian beliefs as they become more exposed to the beliefs of others. We want them to have a real Biblical understanding of their faith as they compare it to what they hear from friends and the world, or at least as much of an understanding as their cognitive ability allows.

Identity: Who Am I?

Most kids are gawky during middle school. As their bodies change they spend a lot of energy comparing themselves to the world and their peers and start deciding who they want to be. They're developing their sense of identity, their self-concept and their self-esteem. It is a challenging time because while they are pulling away from their parents and figuring out their place among their peers, comments made by important adults in the child's life, as well as their peers, could have a great positive or negative effect on their identity and feelings regarding how they see themselves. Low self-esteem develops if there is a discrepancy between a child's self-concept and what they think they *should* be (Harter (as cited in APA, 2002)) or who they think they are versus who they think they should be.

As stated earlier, students have begun noticing how they are physically different from or like their peers. They will also compare their social lives to that of their peers. If, in those comparisons, they feel they are not enough like their peers, they develop low self-esteem which is why they need to be taught to cope with emotional problems and to recognize and manage their emotions. Confirmation can be used to help them develop empathy, resolve conflict constructively, and develop a cooperative spirit. Confirmation teachers can be great encouragers by giving students the opportunity to talk about and help facing problems or fears, listening to their concerns about life, and encouraging them to explore appropriate interests within the context of discussing God, sin, and grace (APA, 2002).

The Media

The media is constantly barging in on the thoughts of adolescents and affecting what they believe about themselves and the world during this time of constant comparison. There is an abundance of opinion and coercion that takes place through mainstream and social media today, and much of it is directed toward adolescents. For students who are looking to belong to a group, it doesn't take but a few in the right group to like or dislike something before they are changing their minds and thinking in a different direction. These new directions may not be permanent, but some may certainly be nerve wracking for the adults in their lives. Music, television/movies, and social media are an increasingly large part of the adolescent's world as they spend an estimated six to eight hours per day or one-third of the day exposed to some form of media. Also youth are increasingly attending to more than one form of media at a time (e.g., conversing on a cell phone with one friend while instant messaging several others on the computer) (Roberts, 2000).

Prior to the media blitz, parents had some idea of what their adolescent was listening to or viewing, especially in their home. However, with the popularity of personal media devices provided by and approved by parents, things have changed. Adolescents have unlimited cell phone use and unlimited connection to the Internet by phone or personal computers in bedrooms. They have access to a huge amount of information without the experience needed to create a mature understanding of it (Elmore, 2012). They are exposed to things without the adult knowing or being able to comment or guide them appropriately (Roberts, 2000), which makes confirmation an ideal place to begin comparing what is acceptable to the world versus what is acceptable to God.

2
COGNITIVE DEVELOPMENT: WHAT ARE YOU THINKING?

What is known today about how the brain develops and works is astounding and aside from the first three years of life, there is no other time when the brain goes through so much change as during adolescence (Elmore, 2012). If you've worked with middle school students you may have experienced a few who are intellectually advanced and yet, have great difficulty dealing with social or emotional situations, both with family and their peers. They argue for the sake of arguing and their logic doesn't always make sense. They don't pay attention very long, they forget what they're asked to do, and they don't consider the consequences of their actions. While these behaviors may have been frustrating parents for years, there is a reason for most them. Here are some basic brain facts (Vawter, 2010).

- The brain isn't completely developed until about 26 years of age.
- The brain develops from back to front, beginning with the primal brain which controls instincts
- The second area that develops is the central brain (amygdala), which deals with emotions and emotional triggers and is usually fully developed by age 16.
- The final area to develop is the frontal lobe (neo-cortex), which deals with executive functions such as goal setting and organization as well as making *wise* choices.
- The brain is constantly rewiring itself to be more efficient.
- Every time something new is learned, a new synapse pattern is created.

- During early adolescence more than 20% of connections made previously are destroyed.

This information is true for all brains and it explains how teenagers make decisions based on emotion often without thinking about consequences. A parent asks, "What were you thinking?" A teen responds, "I don't know." It's not that they don't know what they were thinking, it's that they don't commonly think about consequences.

Children don't develop physically, emotionally or cognitively at the same rate but generally, at this time, they are moving into formal logical operations which includes abstract thinking, problem solving, and mental manipulations with the ability to mentally explore similarities and differences (Biehler & Snowman, 1982). They are learning to discern. Vawter (2010) and the APA (2002) explain a bit of what's going on in those middle school brains during early adolescence.

- Their attention span is about 10 to12 minutes long.
- They begin seeing that *yes* and *no* are not the only answers to life's questions.
- They begin to see that their behavior has consequences.
- They begin to have the ability to consider the future and the idea that they have options.
- They test their reasoning ability and may argue for the sake of arguing.
- They begin developing moral philosophies.

Having an attention span of about 12 minutes doesn't mean that students need to have completely different topics every ten minutes, but it does mean that they can pay attention longer if they have a brain break or focus shift about every ten minutes. The topic may be the same, but the presentation of information or the activity needs to shift into a new direction unless it's something that naturally keeps them thinking. For example, if you're giving about 30 minutes of information via slides and lecture about the early Church, a brain break might be to pause mid presentation to ask "game show" type questions about what was just shared. Following the questions, return to the presentation and provide another brain break in another ten minutes or so. This also reinforces key learning concepts. Another possibility might be to present the information for 12 to 15 minutes and follow that with discussion questions or a group worksheet that gives the students an opportunity to interact with the information in some way or look for support for it by completing a scavenger hunt through the Bible or catechism.

Logical Reasoning—Do They Do That?

Simply put, cognitive development refers to the development of the ability to reason. As young adolescents' reasoning ability gets stronger they may argue for the sake of arguing (APA, 2002). This makes confirmation a good time to challenge those reasoning skills with the understanding that the logic of a young adolescent may not always be sound. As they reason and develop their moral philosophies, they will be processing input from outside the family and the church, and may quote popular, but illogical statistics and sound bites.

When educating young children about the Bible, we tell them the stories and they hear them as facts. Joseph was given a special coat and his brothers sold him into slavery. Fact. As they mature into adolescence, they begin to understand that things are not always black and white. Joseph's relationship with his father caused his brothers to feel jealousy. They sold him into slavery which later saved their lives. The simple story is now more complicated.

Young adolescents are beginning to see that *yes* and *no* are not the only answers to life's questions. Another example is the parable of the prodigal son. It may have seemed simple to them at one time, but as the son who left comes home they may now see, and will most likely believe, that the brother got a raw deal as he was the one who remained faithful to the father and he is not rejoiced over. They will probably not voice that opinion if they think it will be considered wrong, but in their minds it won't seem fair, so it's important to remember that where they see new shades of gray they may need more explanation, though they may not directly ask for it. With all of these thoughts and considerations, their brains are busy creating new synapse patterns as they formalize ideas and opinions of their own.

There are parts of Christian education that are very cognitive. We want students to know some history of the Church and/or the doctrine of their denomination and to know the Bible. This would be the area that is cognitive. We begin educating students for information recall or who did what, when, and where, but that should not be our ultimate goal. We want deeper understanding and the ability to apply what they learn to their lives at their cognitive level. In order to do that, we need to understand that Christian education is also extremely emotional. It's not only about discerning right and wrong based on the Bible. It's about students having faith and knowing that they are forgiven, loved and accepted by a gracious God who gave His Son in their place; being able to share what they believe and *why* they believe it. This is why it's important to ask questions about what they think and believe instead of telling them what to think and believe. This is an executive function, so students may know it, but may not understand it during early adolescence.

Portrait of an Adolescent

Imagine all your students sitting in front of you in your confirmation class. Physically, their bodies are going crazy with hormones and they're very conscious of the physical changes happening to them and all their peers, some that are obvious and some that can't be seen. Along with these physical body changes comes curiosity about sex and the opposite sex, topics which are becoming more real, confusing, and exciting.

Socially and emotionally, they see a bigger world than they did before and are starting to wonder where they fit in. They're beginning to search for a personal identity and are looking to confirm that what they've been told by their parents all these years is correct in the face of a new, broader world view. They're choosing their own friends, relationships are becoming much more complicated, and it's their peers (who have as much life experience and wisdom as they do) to whom they're going for advice.

Cognitively, their brain is in the middle of its development and at the beginning of their journey into reason, logic, and predicting their future. Common sense is not very common at this age. They are *beginning* to understand the many gray areas of life and how their behavior has varying degrees of positive or negative consequences. They enjoy arguing for the sake of arguing, their logic doesn't always make sense and they're *learning* to form opinions based on their own thoughts and experiences as opposed to repeating what they've been told. In many ways, based on what we know about the middle school years, it's a good time to *begin* a faith confirmation program.

Brain and Memory

In his book *Brain Rules*, John Medina (2008), a developmental molecular biologist, shares what he defines as the 12 basic ways a brain works, many of which will boost the religious education experience for middle school youth. While all of the rules are relevant and apply to every brain, there are a few that can be applied directly to confirmation instruction: rules four, five, six, and ten.

Simply stated, rule four is that we do not pay attention to things we find boring (Medina, 2008). For the most part, people assume that this is only true for children, but it's true for every brain as is evidenced by the frequency with which adults change television channels. However, it doesn't mean we need to be more entertaining by turning everything into a game. It means we pay attention to things to which we have an emotional connection or that spark our interest. We like things interesting, meaningful, and/or challenging in some way. The key for confirmation is in helping students create an emotional connection to the material. For example, abortion is a huge political issue. An emotional connection might be made by giving students a detailed scenario where two teenagers are pregnant; one from her boyfriend and another from rape. Is abortion okay? Another example using a less obvious issue such as the Second Article of the Creed might contain a question similar to: "When I count to three, stand up if you agree with this statement: If Jesus died for everyone's sin and all our sin is forgiven, then everyone will be in heaven. One. Two. Three." Challenging a popularly held belief creates an emotional response by hitting a nerve or forcing a reaction to an issue in which they may not be confident.

Rule five is for short term memory and is that we need to repeat to remember (Medina, 2008). Medina says the human brain can only hold about seven pieces of information for less than 30 seconds, but repeating that information will extend that length of time. The best example of this is when somebody gives you their phone number when you don't have anything on which to write it down. What do you do? You repeat it to yourself over and over again until you're able to write it down somewhere. Unfortunately, this is primarily the behavior students practice when learning memory work. The problem is that what they're doing is for short term memory, which is why they rarely remember it longer than it takes them to say it to their parents and get their sheet signed.

Rule six is for long term memory. In order to remember, information needs to be repeated over time, or simply stated, the rule is remember to repeat (Medina, 2008). Being exposed to information repeatedly over periods of time helps move information from short to long-term memory. This is why regular review is valuable. A good example of how long term memory works is the liturgy. Why do I remember parts of the liturgy now even though my church hasn't used that particular hymnal for years? It's because I said it every week for over 20 years. Why do I remember song lyrics the minute they come on the radio for songs I haven't heard since high school? Because when we're teenagers we hear the same songs over and over again almost every day for years. If we want students to remember their memory work, they need repeated exposure to it over time. They should say it to a parent *every* night for a week and then the confirmation teacher should do some kind of random memory review at some point during class where random verses memorized earlier in the year are chosen for them to recite for a small reward.

Rule ten states that vision is more powerful than all the other senses. In other words, a picture really is worth a thousand words. Most people remember things in pictures and even as they read, their brain translates the words into mental pictures (Medina, 2008). Think about Noah. The moment you thought about him your brain flipped through a number of different pictures of an ark, animals, an image of an old man, etc. The concept of Noah is related to those pictures or a brain video. A person will have three times better recall for pictures over words and six times better recall for words accompanied by a visual of some kind (Medina, Vision, 2014). This is why pictures are valuable in books, why lecture slides should have more pictures than words, and why pastors should use pictures in sermons. For example, if pictures of the tabernacle are shown while talking about it, the information will have a much greater effect on the student than a page full of descriptive words or somebody telling them about it. If slides with words on them are used, try to add a picture to help trigger students' memory and help with recall.

3
PLANNING A CLASS: SO MUCH TO LEARN, SO LITTLE TIME!

Confirmation classes usually meet once a week for about 30 sessions ranging from 60 to 90 minutes long. That is not a lot of time, so every minute should be used productively. For this reason, planning how time is used each week is essential. It will keep everyone on task, keep the lesson flowing smoothly, and remind you of what needs to be accomplished. Every teacher has their own style of teaching, so one lesson plan does not fit all, though certain parts of each lesson should always be included. An effective lesson plan is not just a list of topics to be covered, but also briefly includes how and why they are to be covered in order to reach desired goals and help the lesson flow (Enerson, Plank, & Johnson, 2004). Having a written record of what needs to be done also works as a reminder of any special needs you have for that day—for example, special paper, worksheets that need to be copied, music, photos or posters, special books, hymnals, etc.

In planning an effective class it's not only important to consider the goals to be reached, but what the students may already know and whether or not they may have misconceptions about it, which is important when teaching religion as misconceptions may negatively affect faith growth (Enerson et al., 2004). We've all had a few students who show up for confirmation but have not attended Sunday school regularly. This is one area where a Bible reading plan helps, as all students are then reading the same thing at the same time. Some may have read it before or heard it in Sunday school and some not, but that should enrich the discussion.

Believe it or not, students appreciate structure. Knowing what's going to happen provides security so they feel more relaxed when they know what's going to happen in class (Maday, 2008). It is recommended that every class have the same basic structure and include the following three components. (Specific examples of these activities are given in chapter eight.)

Focusing Event or Warm-Up—A focusing event or warm-up gets everyone started on the right foot. It quickly gets the students on task, and when this is done every week, students expect it, and it relieves the teacher from having to redirect the class before it even starts. It also helps focus them on what will be discussed that day or is a quick review of what was discussed last week. A beginning prayer should be said after the warm-up as students will be more settled. If you establish routines and expect the best from your students, you will most likely get it (McFarland, 2000). Warm-up activities should take no more than 5 to 10 minutes.

Lesson Activities—Lesson activities introduce or reinforce information and increase understanding and should be chosen based on which method will help reach stated goals (Enerson et al., 2004). Considering the short time we have with students, all the learning activities should have a purpose. In an hour-long class, not including a warm-up or cool-down, there should be no less than three different learning activities and probably no more than five. Types of learning activities could range from lectures or games to projects, video activities, discussion, or written work. If a Bible reading plan is part of the curriculum, be sure to include at least 15 minutes in the lesson to talk about it and address any questions students might have.

Closing Event or Cool-Down—Closing events or cool-downs wrap things up and remind students of what they learned during class. It's a good time to do a quick assessment and get feedback as to what the students learned. A closing prayer should be said after the closing event.

Middle school students will be more engaged in a task-oriented classroom with structured lessons that relate to their lives when possible (Maday, 2008). Structure and classroom routines make life much easier and research recommends well organized lessons that flow easily from one learning activity to the next to help keep students actively participating and give them less opportunity for off-task behavior (Dinsmore, 2003). A good plan keeps students actively involved and moving in a direction chosen by the teacher.

Having clear directions and varying the presentation is beneficial, as students will respond far better when kept engaged, keeping in mind that being engaged does not mean being entertained (McFarland, 2000). It is when they lose interest that their minds wander, they start thinking about other things to do, and begin talking to their neighbors. If the questions are challenging and the learning activities varied, students will remain interested.

The activities mentioned in this book can be used with any curriculum. If you use a textbook of some kind, this information can be used to develop many simple academic activities that will enhance that text, help engage the students, and make the information more interesting and meaningful to them. Most confirmation textbooks are written so that students can read and respond to the questions provided without teacher input. Unfortunately, with that strategy there isn't a lot of interaction with the material and students may not remember it for very long—not to mention that it's boring. If that type of curriculum is used, I suggest having students read and complete the lesson prior to the class session. That way class time can be used for discussion and more thoughtful learning activities. When confirmation curricula are created they seem to focus more on information, essentially telling them, "This is what you should believe." Instead of that, the lesson section of a confirmation class could be similar to: share Biblical or historical information, provide a vehicle for them to talk and think about it, share more information, provide a different vehicle for them to talk and think about it. Don't tell them what to think or believe. Provide information and ask them what they believe and why they believe it. Remember that their reasoning may be a little off and they may need guidance with further questions or information.

Random Student Choice

It is wise to randomly choose students when asking questions and it is a lot more fun than going down the line one after the other, giving students an opportunity to tune out until their turn. Sometimes teachers get in the habit of choosing their favorite students, or students they know they can count on to respond, more than others. Nobody wants to put students on the spot, but we also want everybody to be comfortable opening up in class, even if their answer isn't always exactly right. When the choice is random, students never know when they'll be called on. When students see that the teacher handles incorrect responses without embarrassing students, they will be more apt to enjoy being called upon randomly.

Names can be written on index cards and/or put on regular playing cards with labels and students or the teacher can "pick a card—any card." Names can also be written on jumbo popsicle/craft sticks and kept in a cup for random selection. Another option is to try one of the many online apps that can be downloaded for free which will allow the computer to randomly draw names while students watch with trepidation or excitement.

Sometimes the physical, old-fashioned way is a bit more convenient and students can participate by actually picking a card. Using an app takes time to load and complete a script, but can also be fun for students. They may even think you're cool for using technology.

There will be multiple opportunities for repetition throughout class. One of a teacher's jobs is to review, repeat, and recap as much as possible. When I teach high school math, there are a few (very few) songs that help students remember formulas (or other pieces of information). The students don't love singing them, but I sing the song every time I write the formula and by the time the test comes around, students are singing the song in their heads. It works!

4
DEVELOPING A CURRICULUM: HOW DO I LEAD THEM THERE?

Developing a confirmation curriculum that is both meaningful and engaging is a lot of work. Most pastors are educated for theology and doctrine, but not education. They know they will teach, but most haven't been given the tools or the skills to develop their own curriculum, though they've been put in a position to do just that. The two most commonly used resources are the Bible and Luther's Small Catechism. In the preface (a letter to pastors and preachers) to Luther's Small Catechism (1986), Luther stated that he realized that the common people were lacking in being able to recite the Lord's Prayer, the Ten Commandments, or the Creed; he worried that without proper education, beliefs would become distorted and the truth of the Gospel lost. He then entreats the pastors and preachers not only to perform the sacraments, but to indoctrinate the people into their beliefs using the catechism. Considering what has been learned about brain development and learning since the 16th century, the Small Catechism is an excellent primary resource, but it is not a curriculum. What we're all looking for is an effective curriculum to intentionally grow understanding and deepen faith in adolescents.

There are some good curricula out there, but most seem either heavy on activity and entertainment, but shallow in the area of content or they are heavy on content and light on academically-engaging activity. Many of the books I've seen are primarily bound worksheets the students complete by filling in a blank and/or completing short answer "discussion" questions. Will students come away with information? Yes, they will. Will they remember it very long? Most likely not. Have students made an emotional/personal connection to it? Again, most likely not. We can do better than mediocre at teaching the most important information they will ever learn. When reviewing or developing a curriculum, the following process is recommended.

Step One: Where Do You Want Them to End Up?

Believe it or not, the best place to start developing a curriculum is at the end (Wiggins & McTighe, 2005). There are three stages of backward design: decide what students should know and/or understand, choose how their learning will be evaluated, and plan appropriate learning experiences. Step one is to decide what they should know by the end of each year. Nobody plans a vacation by getting in the car and starting to drive without deciding where to go or how they will get there first. Most confirmation educators have an informal idea of what they want students to know already as they've been using some kind of curriculum already. They need to write it down and make it formal.

Step Two: What Do You Want Them to Know About Each Topic?

A good resource for constructing goals is Benjamin Bloom's Taxonomy of Verbs, which were created in 1956 and revised in the 1990's by a group of cognitive psychologists lead by a former student of Bloom, Lorin Anderson (Krathwohl, 2002). The taxonomy addresses the three learning domains: cognitive (brain), affective (emotion), and psychomotor (physical) (Krathwohl, 2002). Since we're talking about religious concepts and the students are only 12 or 13 years old, confirmation teachers will most often be dealing with the cognitive and affective domains as they are increasing knowledge and hoping to affect students' attitudes, morals, and how they understand religious concepts that relate directly to their lives. In order to guide students to internalize values and build character based on what they are learning, goals should be written that begin simply with recalling information and grow in complexity of thought and understanding (Clark, 2004).

Notice the words in italics in the example goals as they are from Bloom's rewritten levels of understanding. If a unit is on the Ten Commandments the following goals might be appropriate:

1) The student will be able to ***recite*** the commandments and their meanings.
2) The student will be able to ***describe*** the differences between the two tables in his/her own words.
3) The student will be able to ***interpret and share*** the meaning of each commandment through pictures, words, or actions.

4) In their own words, students will be able to ***discuss*** examples of breaking and keeping each commandment.
5) The student will be able to ***predict*** what natural consequences might occur when people do not follow the commandments.

Keep in mind that a topic or unit may encompass more than one class session. Too many goals for one session may cause the teacher to complete each activity too quickly and will not give the students the chance to interact or reflect on the material in a meaningful way. Given the length of each class, choosing two or three goals for each session is recommended.

Step Three: Assessments—How Will They Show What They Know?

The third step is deciding how you will assess what students know or whether or not they have reached the goals (Wiggins & McTighe, 2005). Many people outside of education think that assessment is about taking tests and quizzes, when actually, there are two types of assessments: formative and summative. A formative assessment is an assessment that is informal and done throughout the lesson or unit while a summative assessment is more of a summary of what's been learned and is usually a final project, test, or formal quiz. Since confirmation classes typically meet once a week, applying formative assessments throughout class and summative only once or twice a year is recommended. Remember that assessments need to point back to the goal and there can be many different assessments possible for each goal.

Formative Assessments

Formative assessments help students develop a deeper understanding of what they are learning far more than summative tests, so that's where we will focus (Clark, I., 2011). While it's difficult, if not impossible, to assess faith or faith growth, it is possible to assess Bible, theological, or doctrinal knowledge and to see if students have an understanding of how that knowledge influences their lives. Possible formative assessments for the Ten Commandment goals listed above might be:

1) **Goal: The student will be able to recite the commandments and their meanings.**
   This goal might relate to a rote memory work requirement and may be assessed verbally or in written form, either in class or at home by the parents. As stated before, it is a good idea to have informal memory challenges throughout the year in order to truly reach this goal.

2) **Goal: The student will be able to describe the differences between the two tables in his/her own words.**
There could be any number of assessments for this goal. One might be a focusing activity or warm-up the week after the information is learned for which students are given a half sheet of paper containing two outlined tablets of stone, and are asked to write a brief description of each tablet on each. For example, on tablet one, a student might write, "Man's relationship with God. Put God above everything, do not misuse His name, and Sunday is His day." As papers are collected, students can share what they wrote. Another might be a closing activity or cool-down that's a quick "round robin" or a "shout out" where the teacher randomly asks students to give an example of a sin that fits in the first or second table. It would also work to give examples of sins and have students shout out which table they fit in, table one or table two. It can be done quickly, like a quiz show, where each student may have more than one turn.
3) **Goal: The student will be able to *interpret and share* the meaning of each commandment through pictures, words, or actions.**
Again, any number of assessments would be acceptable for this goal. It can be assessed as each commandment is examined or after they are all discussed. If a discussion is done correctly, it can be an assessment, but only if every student has a chance to speak and answer a question such as "What does this mean?" in his/her own words. It could also be done in a group setting where students work together to write down the meanings or draw pictures (comic) or come up with actions (mime) or even a rhyme. For example, after discussion, give students ten minutes to work with a partner or as a group to write a rhyme or rap about what that commandment means. If you do it for every commandment, you'll have some pretty cool rhymes that can be printed up and hung around the room or even around the church.
4) **Goal: In their own words, students will be able to *discuss* examples of breaking and keeping each commandment.**
Obviously this assessment is a discussion that can be done in large or small groups. It can then be shared by having students come up with a life example (no names, please) or something they saw in the media to illustrate keeping or breaking each commandment. An assessment such as this one could be done at the end of the lesson or activity on each commandment and would not even seem like an assessment to the students, but lets the teacher know if they have reached the goal based on the examples they give.

5) **Goal: The student will be able to *predict* what natural consequences might occur when people do not follow the commandments.**
This goal might best be assessed after discussion by having students debate ethical dilemmas or deliberate social situations provided by the teacher. Don't forget to choose some very obvious infractions and some that students do every day without even thinking about it as well as a few that might take a little more thought. Having them work in pairs or groups and using white boards to write down examples of natural consequences is also a possibility.

In the examples given above it is clear to see that formative assessments need not be obvious formal events and can be incorporated into the lesson, as part of discussion, or in a focusing or closing activity. Another option would be what teachers call an exit ticket. If five minutes are left in the class after prayer, the teacher could say each student's ticket out the door is to answer a challenge question such as: If God knew He was going to send Jesus to save the people, why did He give them the commandments in the first place? Formative assessments may sound formal, but they really go with the flow.

Summative Assessments

Confirmation doesn't really need summative assessments if formative assessments have been done well, but they can be a nice way to share what students have learned with the congregation and challenge students to think in a holistic way about what they've learned. After all, the point is not just that students are learning, but they're publicly confirming their faith, and it's a great tradition and good experience for them to learn to share it, even if it's indirectly and formally in front of a congregation.

Summative assessments (summary) are usually more formal events that attempt to pull together what the student has learned over time to support the goals. The key to a successful summative assessment is the intentionality with which it is created. Students may be asked to pass a test, create a faith journey poster, write a reflective essay, or create a video or a public service announcement to be shared with the congregation. Many churches have traditions about how this is done. A few options follow.

Test—Tests need to be created carefully. Creating a good test that measures what middle school students know and what they think and believe is not as easy as one might think. They're not familiar with long essay tests, and true/false or multiple choice questions may assess what they know, but not what they're thinking or what they believe. It is possible to use many of the questions in the Small Catechism as test questions as long as students are expected to use their own words in their answers.

Poster—Using posters for summative assessments can be very good if students know exactly what is expected of them. Posters can be developed and professionally printed with empty areas for students to fill in, or students can design their own. If students design their own posters, be sure to give them a list of exactly what needs to be included such as what they believe about God the Father, the Son, and the Holy Spirit and the role of each in a student's life including Biblical support for their beliefs.

Reflective Essay—An essay is a great idea as long as the expectations are age appropriate. How do you get a student to reflect? By asking appropriate leading questions. For example, what do you believe about God and why do you believe it? Allow them to respond to "I believe…" statements and give specific expectations such as using two Bible verses and one life example in support of their choice (see Appendix A). There are three required statements in the example in the appendix, but five statements must be written about. You may limit them, but it's always a good idea to give students choices about what to write.

Video/Public Service Announcement—Students can be super creative with these, but may need to be reminded that their goal is to share what *they* believe. Videos can be created using similar requirements as the reflective essay and the same "I believe…" statements. They can also do "man on the street" interviews asking other people what they believe and discussing how what the student believes is similar to or different than their responses. The video could end with a final statement by the students, "So, this is what I believe and why I believe it." Students may also come up with their own ideas for this assessment. It is recommended that students be given a list of requirements or parameters for this option as well.

Public Witness through Questioning—I know this practice is a tradition, but I have yet to understand its purpose as it's done today outside of it being a rite of passage. Reciting memorized answers is neither a public declaration of a personal faith nor is it a confirmation of what a person believes. Also, public speaking is a great fear for most adults and we not only expect 13-year-olds to do it, but with the added pressure of answering questions. Often, understanding the stress of this event, students are given the answers and may be told which questions they will "randomly" be expected to answer ahead of time. In light of what we now know, perhaps it's time to reconsider this tradition or turn it into something more meaningful than simply surviving a rite of passage.

These are just a few of any number of possible options. The key to making any summative assessment effective is whether or not it challenges students to think about what they believe based on what they've learned throughout the year.

Middle school students need boundaries, guidelines, or rubrics to help them stay focused. Without a rubric (a list of requirements), the student may create a lovely faith journey poster that does not explain their faith journey at all, or a hilarious video that has nothing to do with what *they* believe or why *they* believe it. What is helpful is a written document that lists the items that must be included on the poster, in the essay, or on the video. Beyond those written requirements, students can use their creativity as they choose. Assessments should never be done simply for the sake of assessment. Make them worthwhile or don't do them at all.

Step Four: Learning Strategies

The final step in developing an effective curriculum is to develop lessons and create activities to be done during class. These activities are intentionally created to support the assessments which are, in turn, created to support the goals. The key to this step is to determine what students need to know or what skills they will need to have in order to find success with the assessments and satisfy the goals (Wiggins & McTighe, 2005).

There are a few things to remember when creating lessons and activities for middle school students. As confirmation is not a graded class and there is little extrinsic motivation, students need to find what they are learning interesting and/or meaningful to them in some way. As mentioned earlier, if students have an emotional connection, the learning will have greater meaning to them, but that doesn't mean it has to be fun or entertaining, though it may be perceived as both. It means the activities have to touch an emotional chord with the students. Specific learning strategies are mentioned in Chapter 8 and include large or small group discussion, reading, writing, sharing, an activity, and/or perhaps some use of technology. There may be a time where information is shared through lectures and when that is the case, middle school cognitive development and brain research should be considered and attention paid to the signs of students losing interest which include yawning, talking to a neighbor, or blank eyes (Morgan & Saxton, 1994)—signs I'm sure we've all seen before.

5
THE BEAUTY OF DISCUSSION: TELL ME WHAT YOU KNOW

Once students have taken in the information, it is how they interact with it, internalize it, and integrate it into their lives as they grow and make choices that make it valuable. That's where discussion comes in with regard to Christian education. It's through discussion that we have an opportunity for something to hit an emotional nerve and make a lasting impression.

From a broader student view there are three parts to effective student learning: what students know, how they feel about it, and what they do with it (Morgan & Saxton, 1994). This view fits religious education perfectly. A confirmation student can easily know and recite the Ten Commandments, but if they have a personal emotional connection to them they will have a much greater impact on their learning and their lives. Many of the topics discussed in confirmation can be emotional, as they are directly linked to behaviors and beliefs. A part of confirmation education is not only to impart knowledge about Biblical facts and doctrine but, with the help of the Holy Spirit, to have the information change lives.

One of the most widely understood learning models is that of the three basic learning styles: visual (slides or props), auditory (comments or explanations), or kinesthetic (practice or physical interaction) (Clark, 2004). Once information is presented integrating the three learning styles it can be discussed in a way that allows students to feel something about it strongly enough that they allow it to affect their lives or, in the case of Christianity, for the Spirit to move them in such a way that it changes their lives.

Facilitating Discussion

It is often said that teaching is an art. This is because there are so many things that teachers do that depend on good timing and practiced skills. Facilitating a discussion is one of those things. Effective discussions can provide a number of positive interactions between teachers and students. They provide teachers with feedback, they support a higher level of thinking which helps develop values and change attitudes, they allow participation in learning, and they give students a chance to hear and share different viewpoints (Schurr, 1995).

Many people believe that just having people talking in a group constitutes discussion, but academically that is defined as social talk (Morgan & Saxton, 1994). With social talk there are no agendas, and anybody can introduce any topic in which they have an interest. Academically, discussion is defined as being organized and having a focus and a direction controlled by the facilitator (Morgan & Saxton, 1994). It is an excellent way for middle school students to learn and practice their developing reasoning skills, though adolescents may not open up just because it is expected of them. There are some tricks of the trade to help teachers become skilled at guiding a discussion to a specific point and that will help create an environment where students will share their thoughts and opinions comfortably.

Time to Respond—One of the things facilitators do without realizing it is rush. Asking a question and then waiting for a response can be difficult. You're standing there and they're just looking at you or the floor and saying nothing. They're usually afraid they'll say the wrong thing, so give them time to think and respond. If the teacher jumps in with a response students will wait until that happens every time which will stifle the discussion.

Encourage Without Giving Too Much—Facilitators want to encourage students to respond without giving away too much of the answer. This can happen when teachers prod students by starting an answer for them and hoping they catch on. This leads them to your conclusion. What you're looking for is *their* input or conclusion.

Don't Judge Responses—Try not to tell students they're wrong and be careful of showing disapproval with facial expressions and other body language. You would be surprised what students will pick up from body language.

Speak Less—Sometimes it's easy to forget you're facilitating and get involved in the conversation to the point that you take over to prove your point. Try to remind yourself that you're not lecturing. The point of discussion is to broaden their thoughts and find out what they think in case they need some guidance or more information. Guide them by asking more questions, not directly sharing your opinions.

Model Logical Thought—A nice way to respond to comments where some guidance or correction is necessary is to model your decision making process aloud while you come to a logical conclusion (APA, 2002). Also, try repeating what's already been said to see if they see where the logic fails such as, "Here's what I've heard so far… what do you think?"

Don't Forget Their Age—Try not to challenge students' points of view (APA, 2002). Confirmation students are about 13 years old and perceive the world and God from the point of view of a thirteen year old. Try not to forget this when considering their responses and when trying to explain things.

Give Your Opinion at the End—If you state your opinion too early, they will agree with you and the discussion will be over. Try to get them to come to a conclusion without directly or indirectly stating your opinion until the end.

Want to Hear More?—There are a number of phrases that will help get positive responses when students aren't getting the point. Ask another question to get them to think a little more deeply.

- Why do you think that?
- I need help clarifying. Can you give me an example?
- What do you mean by…?
- I'd like to hear more about that.
- What about…?
- Does anybody else have something to add?

Sometimes teachers have trouble facilitating a discussion because it's a tough group. Students may fall into a predictable pattern where the same vocal students always respond or the group sits looking at you as if you don't speak their language and nobody says a word. If that happens, try to get them moving with one of the following options.

A Beanbag—Start by asking a simple, nonthreatening question that any student can answer and toss the beanbag to a student to answer it. They can toss it back to you or to another student to respond to the same question or the next question. Increase the depth of the questions as the beanbag is tossed around and students will start sharing. Don't be surprised if at one point somebody says, "Throw it to me!" because they have something to share. If they start talking over each other remind them that the person with the beanbag is the speaker and everyone else listens and thinks.

Agree, Disagree, Don't Know—Put AGREE, DISAGREE and DON'T KNOW signs up around the room and have students respond to a statement by standing under their sign. Give them a moment to think, but don't let them talk to their friends before they move and don't forget to ask why they disagree or agree while they're standing under the sign. See if they can change the minds of the others to their opinion and ask anybody who changes their mind why they changed it.

Continuum—Similar to the agree/disagree signs, this strategy uses a continuum from one to five or one to ten along a wall. Students respond to a degree about how they feel or what they think about a statement. Once they pick a number, ask why they chose it and don't let them move without sharing why they're changing their mind. After some information or discussion give everybody a chance to move and explain. Agree/Disagree and Continuum are great when starting with common societal beliefs students may have bought into.

Ultimate Top 3—Have students work in groups to decide the top three or top five (depending on the size of your group). Ask for the three most important reasons why something is true or the five most common idols in our culture, or any similar question. Then have groups discuss why their answers should be the ultimate top three or five.

All of these strategies can be used to get a specific conversation started. Don't be as concerned about whether or not they agree or disagree as *why* they agree or disagree. One of the goals of a discussion is to help students refine and communicate what they think or believe. We want to give them the opportunity to develop their own thoughts, opinions, and feelings based on what they have learned. However, they are young and again, their logic will be off, so let them be challenged and see if they figure it out for themselves before you jump in and correct. There's nothing better than watching the wheels turn in the heads of 13 year old kids as they rationalize and realize things they didn't know before. It's after great discussions that they get in the car and keep talking all the way home!

Bible Reading Discussion

If students are reading the Bible and completing a Bible reading guide, it should be discussed. Never have students read without follow-up discussion. It lets them know the reading is taken seriously and allows them an opportunity to ask questions. Keeping in mind who middle school students are and what they're going through, Biblical accounts can be used in a way that connects with them. In general, but not exclusively, when interacting with friends, boys tend to engage in more action-oriented pursuits while girls spend more time cultivating their relational skills through conversation (Smith, 1997). Use this information to help students connect to and find personal value in Bible stories. Point out the relational versus the adventurous parts of Bible stories to draw students in.

We often lose sight of the fact that the Bible is about real people with real lives and real problems. What kind of faith does it take to command an army to defeat a city by walking around it and blowing horns as Joshua did? How do you feel if you're Leah and you know your husband was tricked into marrying you and really loves your sister? They did not know they were going to be used as examples in God's story of salvation. The people in the Bible were not chosen to be used by God because they were better than everybody else in some way. They were simple human beings with problems and weaknesses like everybody else, who were used by God in spite of those as they lived their lives and made choices every day. Let students have fun with and struggle with the discussion the same way they would about a movie or a novel.

6
SIGNIFICANT QUESTIONS: ALL QUESTIONS ARE NOT CREATED EQUAL

Good questions lead to good discussions and more effective assessments. Creating good questions is another skill that can be developed and practiced until it becomes second nature. Question pitfalls include asking questions that cannot be answered, expecting students to guess what the teacher is thinking, asking obvious questions, and asking simple *yes* or *no* questions. I have seen countless true/false and multiple choice questions in various confirmation curricula quizzes. These questions give little information about what a student understands or thinks.

There are three basic uses for questions. They should either elicit information, shape understanding, or press for reflection (Wiggins & McTighe, 2005). What I have noticed in the church is that we primarily educate for information and not understanding or reflection, which is interesting because every confirmation teacher I talk to will say that he or she wants to know if students "get it." Unfortunately they don't ask questions that will give them that information.

When developing questions, Morgan and Saxton (1994) stipulate a number of learning objectives in order to reach the whole student and promote thinking skills. How a facilitator asks questions can either reinforce what students are learning or have no educational value. I have found far too many adult Bible studies written where there are questions that have no value or do not challenge thinking or reflection. Here is an example from *Witness, Mercy, Life Together* (2011), an adult Bible study:

> Read John 1:1-18. Verse 7 says that God sent John the Baptist *to bear witness about the light (Jesus)*. According to this verse, *what is the purpose of John's witness*? (Emphasis added.)

The answer is clearly to bear witness about Jesus. This is a question for adults, and the answer is literally in the question! If there is no reason to ask a question, or if the answer to a question is obvious, it does not need to be asked. Good questions should be well thought-out and constructed to reach specific objectives. Keeping Bloom's Revised Taxonomy of Verbs (see Appendix B) on hand when developing questions can be helpful. The following are an adaptation of the question objectives developed from Bloom's Revised Taxonomy by Morgan and Saxton (1994) to religious education.

REMEMBERING—Objective: to remember or recall facts or details. Questions that tell what the student already knows or remembers typically begin with who, what, when, or where. These questions are important because without this information, the student has nothing about which to think, talk or reflect.

- Who did Jesus raise from the dead?
- Which king came after David?
- What item went with Joshua and his army to the battle of Jericho?
- Where did Paul go on his first journey?
- Define sin.
- What is an epistle?
- Identify the twelve tribes of Israel.

UNDERSTANDING—Objective: to know what students understand. Questions that show what students understand need to be more complicated as they push the student to think about the facts with more depth. They shape understanding.

- In your own words, tell me what justification means.
- What is the difference between killing and murdering?
- Explain why Jesus needed to be perfect to pay for our sins.
- What do we NOT know about the story?
- What is the purpose of prayer?
- How do you think his life changed?

APPLYING—Objective: to apply information to different situations. Questions that show that information can be applied to multiple situations need to be worded in a way that helps students bring the information into their own lives. These questions press for reflection.

- What would happen if nobody followed the Ten Commandments?
- What examples in your life can you find that show how Christians disrespect Jesus?
- What would you do or say if Jesus asked you why you should be allowed into heaven?
- Why do you think God kept Adam and Eve from re-entering the Garden of Eden?
- How do you know God answers *your* prayers?

ANALYZING—Objective: to support opinion with reasoning and ideas. If the goal is to have a deep understanding of the information, students need to be able to draw conclusions about situations and be able to support them with logical reasons. These questions expect students to show deeper understanding.

- Why do you think God let Eve take a bite of the fruit?
- God is good and everything good comes from God. Give three examples of what the world might be like without the existence of God.
- Who do you admire most in this story and what makes you admire that person?
- What if Noah let some of the people into the ark when it started to rain?
- If God sent His Son to die for everyone, can we assume that everyone will be in heaven? Why or why not?
- What are some reasons people might give for not believing Jesus was the Messiah while He was on earth?

EVALUATING—Objective: to consider the information and be able to make a judgment about it. Students need to be able to summarize information in order to defend an opinion, criticize the opinion of others, or make a valid argument. The answers to these questions may not necessarily be right or wrong, but it is important for them to have an opinion and be able to support that opinion.

- How is the faith of the people of the Old Testament different or the same as those in the New Testament and those of us today?
- If one of the Ten Commandments is more important than the others, which would it be and why?
- What is your opinion of the Pharisees?
- What qualities make you want to admire Peter or Paul more?

- Why was Peter right or wrong to defend Jesus?
- Why does it matter or not matter if your friends know Jesus?
- If it were possible, what would the perfect Christian's life look like?

CREATING—Objective: to take separate elements and create a whole. This objective is to help students take the separate pieces of information and put them together to create a whole thought.

- In your opinion, what are the three most important things every Christian needs to know?
- What would you say to a friend who asked what you believe?
- Choose five words to describe God… Jesus… the Holy Spirit.
- Describe the apostle Paul by the characteristics of his personality. What kind of guy was he?

As questions are developed, it helps to remember the cognitive level of middle school students and that they may struggle a bit with the last three objectives. They're just learning to reason and their logic may be quite off. Don't tell them they're wrong. Guide them. Avoid asking questions students can't answer as well as asking too many questions where they simply have to look back at the reading to copy the answer.

It may take some time before writing good questions comes without intentional thought, but taking the time to enrich the questions in a curriculum is a task well worth the effort.

Bible Reading Comprehension Questions

In most churches, students don't read the Bible. They read selected passages that fit whatever topic they're studying that week. As a result, students miss out on whole stories and on the larger story which is the relationship God has with His people, especially in the Old Testament. If a Bible reading plan is not a part of your curriculum or an expectation for confirmation it's time to think about it.

Reading the Bible is not easy for many adults, much less a 13-year-old. They need to be held accountable and may need help with comprehension in order to discuss it with meaning. There are a number of reasons for this.

- They've heard many of the stories since they were young in Sunday school, so they don't pay very close attention to what they're reading.
- They've read it before and don't pay attention to many of the details, yet as they get older, it's those details that help them grow deeper in understanding.

- They're not held accountable for what they're reading as nobody takes the time to talk to them about it. "Did you read?" "Yes." "Ok."
- Most Biblical accounts aren't really stories, so are somewhat hard to follow. Rather, they're parts of stories with undeveloped characters designed to point to one main character: God.
- The books of the Bible aren't compiled in chronological order, which can make them confusing for students who are used to novels and comic books.

Students need to read the Bible, not bits and pieces taken out of context, not verses or parts of sections chosen to support a topic, not novels where people try to put words in the mouths of the Biblical writers, and not comic books. We don't need to change God's Word or add to it. We need to have them read it. The more they do, the easier it will become for them to understand, even with the confusing ways some of it is worded. At this age they don't need to read all of the prophets and Revelation, but they need to have an understanding of God's relationship with His people from His words.

While developing a Bible reading plan, I included questions for middle school students and high school students. The reading plan is written so that students may read much, but not all, of the Old Testament in one year (33 weeks) with 10 to 15 comprehension questions each week. The New Testament is primarily the Gospels and Acts in one year (33 weeks) with 10 to 15 questions per week, and a third year would include the Epistles. It's not that middle school students cannot answer higher level thinking questions, but their answers will probably be shorter and simpler. We want them to understand what's written before we ask them to think deeply about it. Use these examples to compare different types of questions at different levels for the same passage.

The middle school questions are for students who haven't read each book of the Bible as a whole (not just select passages). They may require the students to go back and reread sections to be sure of what's going on.	The high school questions assume students have already read through each book the first time, so they are higher level thinking questions. They require students to think more deeply or reflect more about how the reading applies to their lives.
Middle School: Genesis 3 – 4	**High School: Genesis 3 – 4**
1. What words or phrases give you an idea of how God enjoyed spending time with His people? What did they do together?	1. Describe God's relationship with Adam and Eve.

2. What was it about the forbidden fruit that made Eve want to eat it?	2. If you could walk with God in the garden, what would you ask Him? What kind of conversation would you have? What would you talk about?
3. What did Adam and Eve receive from eating the forbidden fruit?	3. Describe what it means to have your eyes opened to good and evil. Are yours?
4. When God made it impossible for Adam and Eve to return to the garden, what was He protecting them from?	4. What were Adam and Eve rejecting when they chose to know more than God wanted them to know?
5. Just like Adam and Eve, we make choices to go against God's wishes for us every day. What are some choices you make that take you further away from God?*	5. What was the result of choosing our own desires over God's plan? What are some choices you make that take you further away from God?*

*These questions are the same intentionally in order to assess the difference in answers at each age.

On the bottom of my Bible reading guides I always have an area where students can ask questions about something they thought was odd or that they didn't understand in the reading. If you're going to expect them to do the work, be sure to look them over to address those questions in class discussion.

7
HOMEWORK AND ACCOUNTABILITY: CONFIRMATION PREP

Where confirmation is concerned, homework can be considered confirmation prep. Nearly all confirmation programs include memory work to be done at home during the week, though most have lenient requirements beyond that. Researchers agree that homework increases both achievement and the commitment of students and parents to what is being learned because it requires an investment of time and effort (Van Voorhis, 2011). If this is the case, homework should be considered a valuable part of confirmation. It will increase commitment of students and parents and reinforce its importance beyond one hour a week. Homework should never be busywork. It should have a purpose and be relevant to what is being studied (Van Voorhis, 2011).

Parent involvement in what their adolescents are learning has a positive impact on their success. If the teacher's goal is to have students internalize what they are learning, so that it changes their lives and they can explain it to others, students need to be able to verbalize it and discuss it outside of class (Cripps & Zyromski, 2009). To that end, the following types of homework are suggested as appropriate for confirmation: memory work, Bible reading, unit reading, and family discussion questions.

Memory Work—For the most part, students learn their memory work by saying it a bunch of times in five minutes, so they can integrate it into their short term memory just long enough to write it down or recite it to parents. What they need to do is say it for five minutes every night all week long for it to be transferred into long-term memory. Learning this way should take no more than 10 or 15 minutes each evening.

Whether students recite it in class, write it down in class, or have parents listen and sign off that it has been completed, a form that requires them to say it every night for a week and have parents initial or sign off every night can be helpful (see Appendix C).

Reading the Bible (with a reading guide)—Reading the Bible can be difficult, and having middle school students read passages without having time to process impedes comprehension. This makes it a good homework assignment. A reading guide with appropriate questions (as discussed earlier), geared toward the understanding of basic facts and anticipating vocabulary problems helps with this. This way, when they come to class, students have an understanding of the reading and are prepared to discuss it.

Reading and completing a reading guide should take no more than 30 minutes. The work can either be collected or looked at as students complete the warm-up at the beginning of class. If the teacher prefers not to collect them, they can be inspected as they are checked off to make sure students are giving reasonable responses. Teachers will usually be able to tell pretty quickly which students aren't doing their best work and can then address any questions or concerns.

Unit Reading—Many confirmation programs come with workbooks where the teachers and students read the material in class and go through the questions, answering them together. Consider having students read and answer the few questions before they get to class. Most of the time they will only take about 15 minutes to complete, if students don't do it in front of the television or while texting, as the questions usually refer directly back to the text. That way class time can be used for discussion or deeper interaction with the material. Again, a quick check-off list helps keep track of whether or not students are keeping up with the work.

Family Discussion Questions—Family discussion regarding faith and the Bible should always be encouraged as this is truly how we bring our children up in the faith. Three to five questions prepared for families to discuss each week that relate to past lessons is sufficient. They can be discussed with the whole family during dinner or individually during car rides and might be homework better assigned to the parents and not the students. This provides excellent reinforcement and gives students the chance to share what they are learning and to practice their reasoning skills. It also keeps families involved. Be sure to touch base with the class about how the discussions went, so they know you find the questions valuable. Along with giving a good idea of who's discussing them and who isn't, these questions can be a fabulous transition into the discussion for the day. "What did your family think about….?"

Unfortunately, parents cannot be forced to participate. There are programs where people require a home connection and they get very frustrated if it doesn't work. Some families will do it, but many will not. We have to work with what we have and trust the Spirit to do the rest. Just because we don't see the growth we expect, in the time frame we expect, doesn't mean it isn't there or won't come later.

The most important part of homework for the teacher is the follow through. Nobody will take it seriously if the teacher or pastor doesn't. Given that, it is wise to develop a system to check that students have done their work, which will depend on what is required of them. Keeping track of these things is not about punishment or reward; it's about accountability and responsibility, and lets both students and parents know that the teacher and the church take it seriously enough to hold them accountable.

Accountability

Many pastors have told me that they don't feel they have the authority or leverage to hold students accountable. First, it's the job of the confirmation teacher to do just that. It sends the message that what they're learning is important enough to hold their feet to the fire. If the confirmation teacher or pastor doesn't think the work is important, why would the student and why would their parents? Also, students *need* to be held accountable. At 13 years old they are not yet mature enough to do something because it's good for them. They are the children and we the adults, so we do what's best for them whether they find it valuable, like it, or not.

Finally, there *is* leverage, but we have to be willing to use it. It's not always easy because every teacher wants to be liked by their students. Sometimes they look up at us with the most sincere expressions and share excuses that may or may not be true and we really want to believe them. They're good kids, but they are still kids and will try to get away with things. You are sharing the most important information these children will learn in their lifetime. Stand firm in that knowledge.

What is the leverage and how can confirmation students be held accountable for what they need to know?

You Don't Have to Confirm Anyone—This is a last resort, but it is huge leverage. If students don't participate and show that they understand the material or have thought about it, then why would we want to confirm them? It doesn't affect their salvation in any way; it simply says they didn't do the work. Be up front about it in your first meeting, so that parents know you're serious, and remind them of it if things don't go well.

Having and holding students to expectations should never make you feel bad. It's what's best for them!

Parents—Start with the assumption that parents find confirmation and the work needed for students to be confirmed valuable. Most of the time parents don't know when their kids aren't doing the work, so let them know. If students are supposed to be reading and haven't handed their reading guide in twice in a row, then it's time for a quick email or phone call home. If students get too far behind they'll have trouble catching up.

Rewards Come in Many Forms—Positive reinforcement and incentives often have far greater impact than punishment or consequences. Here are some reward ideas.

- A certificate of perfect memory work given out in front of the congregation.
- A quiz bowl or ultimate memory challenge where people can come and cheer students on as they show off their knowledge. Individual or small teams will work and questions can be taken from their Bible reading guides and/or the catechism.
- Hand out Bible Reading Challenge certificates and add students' names to a "Wall of Fame" of those who've completed all their reading guides. Do it throughout middle and high school to show that learning doesn't end after confirmation.
- If Bible reading punch cards are used, have a reward for every card completed.
- Give informal monthly food/snack rewards in class for those who have both memory and reading requirements done. Some people may disagree with food rewards but they're in middle school and nothing ruins their appetite, so be careful about allergies and don't cave in to pressure or feel sorry for someone who doesn't do the work. No work — no reward!

Verbal Praise—For good or interesting answers or questions on the reading guide, verbal praise can *change a student's attitude completely* toward the Bible or unit readings. Let students know their answers are read by going through them and commenting on good responses. There's no need to comment on every student every week, and try not to praise the same students over and over or leave anybody out for too long. Confidence will grow every time a student hears, "John asked a good question on his reading guide this week. Let's talk about it."

8
CLASSROOM MANAGEMENT: SET YOURSELF UP FOR SUCCESS

Most people perceive classroom management as controlling the behavior of students, but research confirms that effective teachers manage a classroom as opposed to controlling the behaviors of students (Englehart, 2012). Sometimes confirmation teachers think they shouldn't tell students *no*. After all, they're only here an hour and a half and we want them to come back, right? Wrong. It's perfectly acceptable to tell a student *no* and stop inappropriate behavior. Based on research and personal experience, the following will help up front with classroom management: set the climate, set expectations, plan your time, and build relationships.

Set the Climate

From what's on the walls to the teacher's tone, the atmosphere created in a classroom can positively affect class mood and therefore behavior (Dinsmore, 2003).

Plants and Color—There is a reason people go to the trouble of make waiting rooms and business offices more comfortable and welcoming. When people are comfortable, they relax and open up more. This also applies to classrooms. Having stark white walls with nothing on them does not set a welcoming, relaxing tone.

Pictures and Posters—When students are bored they take a mental break and look around the room. It's to the teacher's advantage to give them something to look at that also makes them think and supports what is being taught. Inspirational and informational posters work well for this. Try a few posters with Bible verses, posters of prayers, or character building posters.

Circle Up for Discussion—Discussion goes more smoothly when students sit in a circle as opposed to sitting behind tables or desks (Dinsmore, 2003). Be careful not to take it too far. Lounging around on couches while eating snacks will cause them to disengage enough that it may be a challenge to keep them on task.

Attitude and Tone—The climate of a class also includes the attitude of the teacher. A fair classroom manager is a respected classroom manager. Leave all your problems at the door, be yourself, and don't take things too seriously or personally. Be ready to laugh when they're funny, because they are *really* funny!

Model the attitude that confirmation instruction is the beginning of a journey that ends when we meet Jesus face-to-face, reading the Bible is cool, and being in class is a privilege. While there is a lot to learn, we hope students have some fun in the process. The teacher's job is to be the guide on this faith building journey. There is power in having a sense of humor, and it goes a long way when dealing with adolescents (McFarland, 2000).

Set Expectations and Keep Them High

The expectation of appropriate behavior should be set right at the beginning of the year and put in written form so it can be shared with parents and students. What is shared doesn't need to be complicated and shouldn't be too long. It simply needs to state that appropriate behavior is expected and problems will be dealt with as necessary. Listing too many rules is confusing and may make the teacher's ability to manage more difficult (see Appendix D).

Middle school students need consistency of rules and expectations (Vawter, 2010). Having a well thought-out management or discipline plan in place before the first class session can alleviate on-the-spot behavior decisions and give everybody an idea of what to expect (Obenchain & Taylor, 2005). Most importantly, it gives teachers an opportunity to consider how they want to respond to specific behaviors. A lot of this isn't a problem if a class is small, but every once in a while there's one challenging student who pushes, and it's good to think about a few things before we have to act or overreact. Some suggest that if students are involved in developing a covenant of rules and their consequences that they will be more likely to follow them. I prefer simple rules based on common sense that center around respect:

> **Respect for the Learning Environment**—This may include being on time, not disrupting class, not using electronic devices, or not eating food without permission.
>
> **Respect for Property—**This may include no gum, not sitting on or writing on tables, and taking care of books.
>
> **Respect for Each Other**—This may include speaking to and treating each other well, not borrowing without asking, keeping your hands to yourself, and using appropriate language.

Confirmation teachers don't need to come up with a bunch of rules and consequences. Students know which behaviors are appropriate and which are not, but it's in their nature to try to get away with things.

Consequences for specific behaviors should be logical and based on the offense. Always be ready to follow through on what you say you will do. For example, if a student is messy with food that student should have to clean up after him- or herself, and perhaps after the whole class. If students write on the table, which they often do without thinking, they should clean all the tables after class or before the next class. If a student leaves a bunch of ripped-up paper on the floor, he or she can clean it up and empty the trash cans in other classrooms as well. If you tell a student you're going to talk to their parent, be sure to do it. Credibility is lost if the student is allowed to talk the teacher out of a consequence, and the first student who is held accountable sends a message to the whole class that you mean business. Teach them to be responsible young people and treat the church building and each other with respect. It is suggested that making reading the Bible or learning more memory work not be used as a consequence. Those activities should never be considered a punishment.

Have the same expectations and show them consistently to all students (Englehart, 2012). This shows that you don't show favoritism and that the same rules apply to all students. The last thing you want is for students to think you have a favorite. There are times when students have said, "I'm your favorite, right?" "Yes, you are." Another student says, "But I thought I was your favorite!" "Yes, you are." For years they have all been my favorite, even the ones who drive me crazy. Dealing with students openly and honestly shows respect. If you show it, you'll get it.

Zero Tolerance

Disrespect seems to run rampant among adolescents today. It seems they have been allowed to feel they have a right to speak their minds whenever they want. It doesn't help that when they are verbally disrespectful they often get positive feedback from other students. Students who are mean or disrespectful to the teacher or other students should be expected to make it right. Notice that all the options listed below include students taking responsibility for their behavior.

"I'll Wait…"—As mentioned earlier, adolescence is a time when students are very social and random conversation can be a problem. Teachers should never share information when they don't have all of the students' full attention. The best way to handle this situation is to stop talking when students start. Simply stop, look at the offending student(s), and say, "I'll wait." It usually only takes a few seconds before they realize they're holding up the class and stop talking. If they don't get the hint, ask, "Is there something important we can help you with so we can continue?" Having a sense of humor at this time works well until they get the idea that they shouldn't talk when you are.

Step Out of Class—Sometimes it's necessary to ask a disrespectful student to step out of class, but do not stop class to deal with it. If it's not possible to deal with the problem immediately, pause just long enough to ask the student to sit in the hall and let him or her know that you will be out to talk in a moment. Once you have a chance to speak to the student, the discussion should sound something similar to: "You seem to be having a bit of trouble today. What's going on?" Let the student explain and then say, "I can't have you behaving like that in class; what can you do to fix it so we can get you back in there?" If the student doesn't have an answer, give him or her a little more time to think about it in the hall. No student should be out in the hall more than five to seven minutes. If that happens put a chair in the back corner of the room where the student can sit away from all other students with the understanding that a parent will be notified if they cannot figure out how to improve their own behavior.

If the problem is between two students, separate them and talk to them about it after class. Let them know that if they cannot sit together and behave then they cannot sit together. Students should apologize to the teacher and/or their peers for disrupting class. Do not let them off the hook.

Dear Teacher—After giving a couple of warnings (but no more than three) or if they haven't been able to come up with a response while sitting in the hall, another option might be to require them to write two paragraphs about why they should be allowed to stay in class when they can't behave, and what their plan is to fix their behavior problem. This is especially appropriate for students who have recurring problems.

Three Strikes—Have a three strikes rule. Simply hold up one finger so the student knows he or she is at strike one. On strike three, depending on the offense, the consequence might be sitting out in the hall, and then in order to return to class the following week, two written paragraphs about what it means to be disrespectful, and what will be done to correct the behavior.

Plan Class Time Wisely

What most teachers don't realize is that 95% of behavior problems can be solved by using class time effectively. Planning keeps teachers from wasting what little valuable time we get with our students and it keeps them out of trouble. Using opportunities for movement, so they don't sit in a chair listening through the whole class can help too. Look back at the chapter on discussion for examples on how to incorporate movement into discussion time. One of the keys is to make sure you flow easily and quickly from one learning activity or topic to the next. In order to do that, be as prepared for class as possible, so class is not disrupted by leaving to make copies or running to get a forgotten book. Anytime you pause, they pause, and when they pause, they immediately become social and it takes time to get them to regroup.

Transition after 15 Minutes—With the attention span of a middle school student at 10 to 12 minutes, it's easy to tell when they get bored and have stopped paying attention. It does neither teachers nor students any good to keep going down the same path when that happens. Constantly and informally assess the interest level of the students (Morgan & Saxton, 1994). Signs of disinterest include looking at everything in the room except you, talking to a neighbor, yawning, putting heads down, not responding to questions or comments verbally or physically, and unfocused eyes as if they have tuned out.

Don't Involve Parents—Involving parents too soon sends a message that the teacher can't handle simple behavior problems. If there was a problem with a student during class, let a parent know without making it a big deal. Try a quick comment as the parent picks up the student such as, "Bye [Name]. Hopefully things will go a little better for you next week. See you Sunday!" With that, the parent conversation begins in the car. If a problem persists, and as a last resort, sit down with the parents and student and let them know that valuable information is being missed due to behavior. If another conference is warranted, let them know that the child may not be confirmed. This should always be a last resort.

One Squirrelly Student—Every once in a while a student will fidget. They may be ADD or ADHD, or maybe they just can't sit still, listen, and process. Sometimes it works to give a squirrelly student a paperclip to fiddle with while taking notes. I don't know why it works, but sometimes keeping a hand busy helps them focus. Or perhaps they need a few moments to pull themselves together. If necessary, ask the student to step outside for a moment and after a few minutes check to see if he or she is ready to return. After some time with a squirrelly student a teacher may develop a rapport and be able to curb behavior with a pointed look and by asking, "Do you need to step outside?" The student will straighten up and won't need to leave.

Develop Relationships—The greatest deterrent to bad behavior is developing relationships with students. They are motivated to please people they like. Try to be yourself, show interest in them beyond the classroom, and talk to them enthusiastically about what is happening in their lives. This will build mutual respect (McFarland, 2000). Spending time developing sincere relationships with students may simplify your classroom management to something as simple as an unhappy look in a student's direction. Remember that adolescents are looking for adult role models; they are developing and solidifying their morals and beliefs, and trying to figure out who they are. Confirmation teachers can both deter inappropriate behavior and play an important role in that process if they build relationships with their students.

9
LEARNING STRATEGIES: INTERESTING + MEANINGFUL = EFFECTIVE

It always helps to have a few things prepared and readily available for each class, so valuable time is not used for copying or fetching. For example, I don't like it when students rip off small pieces of "scratch" paper to use and hand in. I end up with all kinds of crazy sized pieces of paper that are easy to lose. Instead, I have pastel paper cut into quarters or halves and have those ready for quick quizzes, warm-ups, cool-downs, or any other activity where they need a quick piece of paper. I use pastel so that it's not so dark that it's difficult to see the writing and colored, so that it doesn't get lost on my desk. Have a copy center cut one ream in half and then cut one of the half stacks into quarter sheets and there'll be enough paper for a number of years.

Focusing Activities or Warm-Ups

If the warm-up requires a piece of paper or if it's a crossword or another type of worksheet, have a designated place to put them, so students can pick them up on their way to their seats. Have directions on the board or screen to keep from having to repeat them each time a student enters the room. Let students know that they're supposed to do these activities *on their own* unless otherwise specified. Having a warm-up will help classes begin smoothly every week.

Pre-Quiz—A short quiz can be really helpful in giving an idea of what students think or know about the topic *before* class gets started. The same quiz can also be used as a cool-down to see how much better they do after the lesson.

Photo Response—Have a cartoon or photo displayed that has something to do with the lesson that day and have students jot down a response to it.

Coffee Cup Theology—There are tons of misused Bible verses and quotes inappropriately attributed to the Bible flying around social media. Put one of them up for students to respond to: What's wrong with this phrase, quote, or verse? Biblical or not Biblical?

Quick Quiz—Put together a few review questions on what was learned last week. Make them thinking or opinion questions as opposed to true/false or multiple-choice and be sure to give the answers either right before class starts or before they go home. They don't have to be graded, but it never hurts to keep track of who's getting them right or wrong as they'll help shape the lesson or follow up discussion.

Correct Me If I'm Wrong—Write down two truths and a lie about a previous lesson and have students figure out which are true and which are not. This can also be done with three truths and two lies or any combination of statements. Make them tough!!

Take a Poll—Every once in a while it can be beneficial to poll students about something they're going to learn that day. After all, we're all about statistics these days. Responses can be collected and used later to see if opinions have changed. To make things really interesting, ask them some questions found in Barna or Gallup polls about Christians and find out what they believe. It's another great way to transition into the topic of the day.

Memory Check—Have students write down the memory work for the week. If they already have parents sign off, have them write down memory work from a few weeks or a month ago as well.

What Does This Mean?—Have students define a couple of terms. Don't choose so many that they can't be done in about five minutes—no more than three are suggested.

Consider This—Write up a scenario similar to what somebody in the Bible faced, but make it fit their lives today and have them respond. It helps them put the actions of Biblical characters into perspective and shows them that their lives and choices are not so different today.

Who Am I?—Provide clues that describe a prophet, Bible character, or well-known person in Church history to see if the students can figure out who it is based on the clues. If they can't figure it out before time is up give them a few more obvious clues right before class starts.

Music—Have hymn or contemporary song lyrics copied for students to pick up as they arrive, and ask them a few questions about it or have them choose their favorite phrase and share why they like it. It might also be fun to have music playing as they enter to introduce them to worship music through history.

Lesson Activities

As discussed earlier, there are a number of factors that go into creating interesting and meaningful lessons for adolescents with the goal of moving them from factual knowledge and recitation to a deeper understanding and internalization of religious concepts. All activities should be created keeping in mind the physical, emotional and cognitive development of young adolescents.

- They enjoy interacting with each other.
- They are able to see that life is made of up shades of gray.
- Friends are having greater impact on their choices.
- They are learning and enjoy practicing their reasoning skills.
- Their friendships are becoming more complicated.
- They are beginning to develop their own sense of identity and moral standards.
- They are very aware of their changing bodies.
- Their attention span is ten to twelve minutes (especially when presenting new information).
- They learn more when an emotional connection is made to the material.

Considering this information, these and similar ideas can be used to enhance your teaching time.

Lecture or Discussion Outline—There is nothing wrong with sharing information with students through a ten minute lecture, but in middle school they have difficulty deciding what's important enough to write down and what isn't. One way to help them learn the skill is to provide an outline or a list of questions that will be asked during the lecture or discussion. This keeps students focused, and as they complete the outline, essential phrases can be repeated aloud, which aids in memory retention. The key is to pause for them to complete the outline and also to ask them questions as information is shared. It is not a good idea to give them a complete outline to save time. They won't go over it at home. Having them search for a missing word in a sentence or phrase is also not a good idea, nor should they copy phrases directly from a slide while you talk. If given the opportunity, they'll write before they'll listen, so have them write first and talk about what they've written when their pencils stop moving.

Graphic Organizers—A graphic organizer is a picture somewhat like a flowchart or Venn diagram that is used to help students organize information such as character traits or timelines. These would be helpful when discussing things like the Old Testament timeline of kings, people and events in the life of Jesus, or the characteristics of God. They should be created ahead of time, and as students read or listen they complete their graphic organizer to help them keep the details of the story or information organized. These organizers could be used instead of an outline for some topics. (See Appendix E.)

Lesson or Reflection Journal—Students can keep a journal of what they learn every week. Take five to ten minutes at the end of class to write about something or have them do it at home. It would be wise to give some thought to what they will respond to before class. For example, when studying parables, they can write down the meaning of each parable and how it relates to their lives. When studying the first petition of the Lord's Prayer, they can reflect on ways in which their friends and the world no longer use God's name appropriately and why that's a problem. They will need guidance as to what to write about as they are not yet good at reflecting on their own.

Another option is to give them two options from which to choose. They choose one and write a paragraph (no less than five sentences). Along with the example listed in cool-downs with regard to the fifth commandment, you might add: "God wants what's best for us in our earthly relationships. Think about a time when a couple of your friends were fighting with each other and said hurtful things to each other. How did it make you feel? How does it affect your relationship with each of them and the rest of your friendship group?" Expect them to respond in their own words, using complete sentences and correct capitalization and punctuation.

Technology—Technology provides a variety of tools that need to be used appropriately for the age group. It should be used to engage the students and create a stronger connection to the material. Pictures, videos, or other visual aids have a tendency to help create emotional connections with the material. The Glo Bible is a great resource for this purpose. Technology can also be used to introduce students to contemporary Christian music and beautiful old hymns as well.

Maps—If we want students to learn about the regions discussed in the Bible, we need to give them a map to fill out as each region is mentioned. For example, have them draw their own map of Paul's journeys and label interesting occurrences that happened along the way. This gives them a great visual for retelling the journey. For the warm-up the following week, hand out blank maps to be completed and see how much they remember. If they have trouble, give them a list of the cities or areas and see if they can put them in the right place on the map. If you need a resource, try *Reproducible Reference Maps* (Concordia Publishing House). Rose Publishing provides a number of books of Bible charts, graphs, and maps as well.

Ethical Dilemmas—Adolescents love to grapple with moral and ethical dilemmas (APA, 2002). Allowing them to do so, with adult guidance, will help them both refine their belief system and be able to verbalize what they believe in a world where so many people disagree with Christian beliefs. Creating ethical dilemmas around moral and ethical issues would be a great activity with which to end a unit or, if students really enjoy them, choose one dilemma that relates to the topic to discuss as a cool-down every week. If you're having a problem coming up with something, watch a little popular television and you'll have plenty of examples of teenagers making poor choices.

Debate—Debate is a great activity, but middle school students have little experience with it. Traditionally, debate is supporting opposite sides of the same issue. They will need to be shown how it works or it will become two groups yelling their opinions at each other. Also, let them know exactly what constitutes support for an argument and remember that their logic may often be faulty. Give them a specific amount of time to work in groups to determine the pros and cons of an argument and who will speak when. There may be issues that students disagree with, but they will grow as they become more familiar with how those on the other side of an issue might respond.

Verbal Charades—This is a fun activity to reinforce vocabulary. Students pull terms out of a bowl, bucket, or hat and describe them in a way that allows other students to guess what they are to earn points.

Closing Activities or Cool-Downs

Cool-downs can be as simple as a quick round robin where each student verbally shares one thing they learned or found interesting during class, or a summary of what was learned, in only a few sentences. Some of the warm-ups can also be used as cool-downs, but they are about wrapping up what was learned during that class. A closing activity should take no more than five or ten minutes, and some can be done either verbally or in written form.

Quick Quiz—Have students answer a few review questions on what was talked about that day. Again, make them thinking or opinion questions as opposed to true/false or multiple-choice and be sure to give the answers at some point during the next class. It's usually best to return papers from the previous week during the warm-up. They need the feedback and you can use them as a formative assessment to show if they understand the material.

Take a Poll—As mentioned in the warm-ups, a poll can be helpful both at the beginning and/or the end of class. Don't forget to collect the responses and check them out. There may be something to be revisited later.

What does this mean?—This is the same activity that was mentioned earlier as a warm-up, but as a cool-down it can be used to recall terms learned that day.

Questions—Have students write down two questions they have about the topic discussed that day before they leave. This will tell you if they've thought enough about the topic of the day to have more questions about it, or if they're curious. If they can't come up with their own (they're 13 years old and just want out), try giving them a prompt.

Recap—Have students share one thing that was talked about that they didn't know before that day and one thing they would like to know more about.

Reflection Journal Entry—Take the last five to ten minutes to have students respond to a journal question. Ask a higher level thinking question.

For example, if you were talking about the Fifth Commandment, you might have them reflect on the following prompt: Think about a time when a sibling or parent got really angry. Did they say something mean? How does it change the personality of your family when somebody is really angry or upset? Another option regarding the Ninth Commandment might be: How do you think it would affect somebody's life if they spend too much time wishing they had somebody else's things? Check the journals once in a while to hold students accountable.

The 5 W's—Have students complete the 5 W's about what was studied that day: Who, What, When, Where, and Why.

Brain Break

Every once in a while, when you've been going on about something for a while and students have hit their focusing limit, try a brain break. It's a brief activity to change focus for just a few moments. There will be some perfect moments to try these.

Bible Culture Corner—The culture of the people of the Bible is foreign to confirmation students and they find other cultures interesting. It helps them to identify with the people if they have an understanding of how they lived and the rituals and traditions they found important. For a quick brain break, try giving them some cultural information. If you need a resource try the *Complete Bible Discovery Guide* (Concordia Publishing House). A document camera can be really handy for things like this and one can be purchased for about $100, which is a good investment for all the other things for which it can be used.

Cartoon—There are a number of funny historical cartoons that can be found online that might fit the lesson of the day and give students a good laugh. They can also be placed at the end of a lecture and used as a signal to students that the slides or notes are over.

Coffee Cup Theology—This one is mentioned in warm-ups, but can also be used as a brain break if the verse or quote fits the lesson.

Memory Challenge—At an appropriate time or as a transition, pause for a quick memory challenge. Use jumbo craft sticks or cards to randomly choose a student. The same method can be used to choose what they'll recite as well. Don't choose anything they were to recite for that week. This will give them incentive to keep going over their memory work throughout the year. Give a simple food reward as incentive. It's more motivational than you think and middle school students love that!

Miscellaneous Ideas

Say It with Me, Folks!—As stated earlier, according to John Medina's (2008) *Brain Rules* when students have to repeat a concept, it sticks with them longer. Strategies that support this are having students put something in their own words, having them repeat something back after you have said it, or having them summarize what was just said. These things can be done verbally or in written form during class. I regularly have students repeat something after me. They think it's ridiculous, but they know that when I say "Say it with me folks…" that I won't stop until they do and the next time it will be "with feeling now…" until they do it again. I use this strategy when I have one important concept that I have condensed into a single sentence such as "I cannot believe in Jesus without the help of the Holy Spirit." Good teachers know their job is to remind, repeat, and recap as many times as they can.

Sometimes it's even better to have students paraphrase or summarize something themselves, especially if they need some common phrases to help answer questions their friends or acquaintances might have about why they believe. It's moments like this when students can work together to help each other come up with how they would respond to people in their own words that really helps things stick with them. Nobody wants to respond to a question by staying, "I don't know. That's what my pastor told me."

Small White Boards—Small white boards can be used to have students work in pairs to rewrite something in their own words and then share it with the class, to answer questions where a list might be involved, when you want students to share their answers to a question at the same time, to respond to brainstorming, top three or top five, or when playing a game. For example, if you ask an agree/disagree question, have students write an *A* or *D* on the white board and keep it hidden until the signal is given for them to show their answers at the same time.

Catechism Questions—The questions and answers in the Small Catechism are a valuable tool that many adults have forgotten exist. The questions and Bible verses in the back of the catechism can be used to create an activity where pairs or groups of students match the Bible verse with the question. This activity requires them to become more familiar with the questions and their answers. In order to match them they have to think about how the question and the verse relate to each other; it helps them become familiar with the Biblical support for what they believe, and it gives them confidence for when they share their faith. They may not be able to recite each verse, but they confidently know it's Biblical, and if necessary, can look back and find it in the catechism.

Another option is to provide a statement of faith and have them use the catechism to find the verses that support it or switch it up and have them find the statement of faith that the verse supports. It's simple to copy a few pages of the catechism and cut the verses apart so that students can't tell the category in which they were located.

Movement—This was discussed earlier to help generate discussion and can also be done as a brain break if students start losing focus. Fist-to-five is also a way to get students physically involved. It is used as a scale vote. Students close their eyes, to keep them from seeing how their friends are voting, and a fist is zero and means "I do not understand, do not want to do it, or I vote no" and a five means "I completely understand, I definitely want to do it, or I vote yes." Any vote in between the two is along the zero to five scale.

Notecards—Notecards can be used for many things, but my favorite use of them is for memory work. Hand out a single ring binder clip to help students keep them all together and they'll have a nice "flip book" of everything they need to memorize. This way they can review verses throughout the year to successfully participate in memory work challenges as they come up. They should write them down themselves as it aids in memorization.

Question Jar—A question jar is simply a jar available to students that allows them to ask anonymous questions. Students often have questions they do not want their peers or their family to know they are asking. The question jar is a perfect answer to that. Students do not like to be the first to ask a question, so I have found that if I put a few questions in myself, it gets the ball rolling and they feel more comfortable. This may be helpful when discussing issues such as adultery, lust, women in the church, homosexuality, and coveting. Of course, we never know what students will be curious about.

Lesson Plan—As stated earlier, using class time wisely is to the teacher's advantage as it keeps students on task, keeps the class flowing smoothly, and also keeps the teacher focused and moving toward the chosen goals. Each strategy should be considered a vehicle used to move the students down a path to greater understanding. Pulling everything together can be a lot to remember. Creating a simple form of some kind to remember all the pieces to be covered throughout the lesson is recommended (see Appendix F).

These are a few of the many ways to help students interact with the Word of God and the doctrine of the church. (For a list of all the activities see Appendix G.) Our goal in teaching confirmation is to help students think about their faith in ways that will help them understand it and further share it with the people in their world. My goal is to help you do that to the best of your ability. To God be the glory!

> Jesus went through all the towns and villages, teaching in their synagogues, proclaiming the good news of the kingdom and healing every disease and sickness. When he saw the crowds, he had compassion on them, because they were harassed and helpless, like sheep without a shepherd. Then he said to his disciples, "The harvest is plentiful but the workers are few. Ask the Lord of the harvest, therefore, to send out workers into his harvest field." Matthew 9:35-38

APPENDIX A
REFLECTIVE ESSAY REQUIREMENTS SAMPLE

"I Believe..."

Confirmation Reflection Essay

The goal of the confirmation essay is to think about what you know about the Church and your relationship with Jesus Christ and how it all fits into your life. We should all ask ourselves these same questions every once in a while, if for no other reason than to remind ourselves who we are in relationship to our Creator and Redeemer. This is your moment. "I know what I've been told and what I've been taught about God and the church. Now, **WHAT DO I BELIEVE and WHY DO I BELIEVE IT?"**

Step 1: Think about it. The only way reflection works is if you really take the time to think about it. What do you believe about God? Jesus? The Holy Spirit? How do they fit into life? How do they fit into YOUR life? Can you see them there?

Step 2: Choose 5-7 belief statements. The first three (3) are required. You must use *at least* two (2) Bible verses and one (1) life example to support each "I believe…" statement. Choose your top 10 belief statements at first, then think about them and narrow down your choices. What has happened in your life and on your faith journey to bring you to this belief? (You do not need to choose from this list. You can come up with your own and have them approved.)

REQUIRED

- I believe God exists and is the creator of the universe.
- I believe the Holy Spirit works in my life.
- I believe that Jesus was the Christ and He suffered for my sins and redeemed me.

YOUR CHOICE (below are *examples*):

- I believe God is love and much, much more.
- I believe that sometimes life is hard and perseverance will get you through.

- I believe a sense of humor is one of God's greatest gifts.
- I believe my family has influenced who I am and what I believe.
- I believe my faith affects other people in my life.
- I believe faith is the most important thing I have.
- I believe in miracles. I believe in tragedies. I believe in hope.
- I believe God can make good things out of bad.
- I believe in living my faith.
- I believe choosing friends carefully is important.
- I believe everything can be forgiven.
- I believe that faith in God can change anybody's life for the better.
- I believe a relationship with Jesus helps me find my way through life.

Step 3: Write!

Introduction—Your introduction should introduce you to your readers and tell them why you chose the belief statements that you did. (Do not say "because the pastor made me!")

Belief statements—These should include supporting information. Each paragraph begins "I believe..." and tells why you believe it and ends with the Bible verses and your life example.

Conclusion—This is how your life has changed because of these beliefs. This is how you intend to live because of these beliefs.

> For the teacher: You might want to hand this information out at the beginning and middle of the year to make sure students are really thinking about it. I've seen some really great "I believe..." statements, but they come from personal experiences. When the students are done, they can choose a statement to share with the congregation and a photograph that explains it and a slide show can be created (include music) before or after a worship service. I suggest sharing the statements without the author's name as some of them may be extremely personal.

APPENDIX B
BLOOM'S TAXONOMY OF VERBS (REVISED)

Remembering	Understanding	Applying	Analyzing	Evaluating	Creating
Can the student recall or remember information?	Can the student explain ideas or concepts?	Can the student use the information in a new way?	Can the student distinguish between the different parts?	Can the student justify a choice or decision?	Can the student use the information to create something new?
Define Duplicate List Memorize Recall Repeat Reproduce State	Classify Describe Discuss Explain Identify Locate Recognize Report Select Translate Paraphrase	Choose Demonstrate Dramatize Employ Illustrate Interpret Operate Schedule Sketch Solve Use Write	Appraise Compare Contrast Criticize Differentiate Discriminate Distinguish Examine Experiment Question Test	Appraise Argue Defend Judge Select Support Value Evaluate	Assemble Construct Create Design Develop Formulate Write

APPENDIX C
MEMORY WORK SIGN-OFF SHEET SAMPLE

Memory Work	Due On	Day 1	Day 2	Day 3	Day 4	Day 5	Day 6
		Parent Initials					
Books of the O. T.	Wed 9/14						
Books of the N. T.	Wed 9/21						
All Books of the Bible	Wed 9/28						
Introduction to the Lord's Prayer and meaning	Wed 10/5						
First Petition of the Lord's Prayer and meaning	Wed 10/1						
Etc.							

APPENDIX D
DISCIPLINE PLAN SAMPLE

A discipline plan can and should be written into a syllabus and can be relatively simple.

Expectations

1. Students **will** attend class sessions and be prepared.
2. Students **will** worship *regularly* with their parent(s), even during the summer.
3. Students **will** attend Midweek Advent/Lenten services.
4. Students **will** attend 7th or 8th grade Sunday School.
5. Students **will** have fun and will learn a lot about Jesus and His Church!

It goes without saying that parents are expected to worship regularly and are encouraged to attend Bible study as well. Parents are the single greatest influence on the habits of their children, and good habits are formed now!

Appropriate Behavior

We're here to learn about the life, death, resurrection, and teachings of Jesus, and respectful behavior is expected. There are three basic rules.

1. **Respect for the Learning Environment:** Be on time, do not use electronic devices, and do not eat food without permission.
2. **Respect for Property:** No gum allowed, do not sit on or doodle on tables.
3. **Respect for Each Other:** Treat each other positively, do not borrow without asking, keep your hands to yourself, and use appropriate language.

If learning is being disrupted, appropriate steps will be taken to remove the disruption. If this occurs, the hope is that the student will be asked to adjust his or her behavior choices. If not, you and your child can talk about it and correct the problem so it doesn't happen again.

APPENDIX E
GRAPHIC ORGANIZER SAMPLES

The graphic below is for the seven "I am…" statements made by Jesus. Students can add the words and pictures to help them remember.

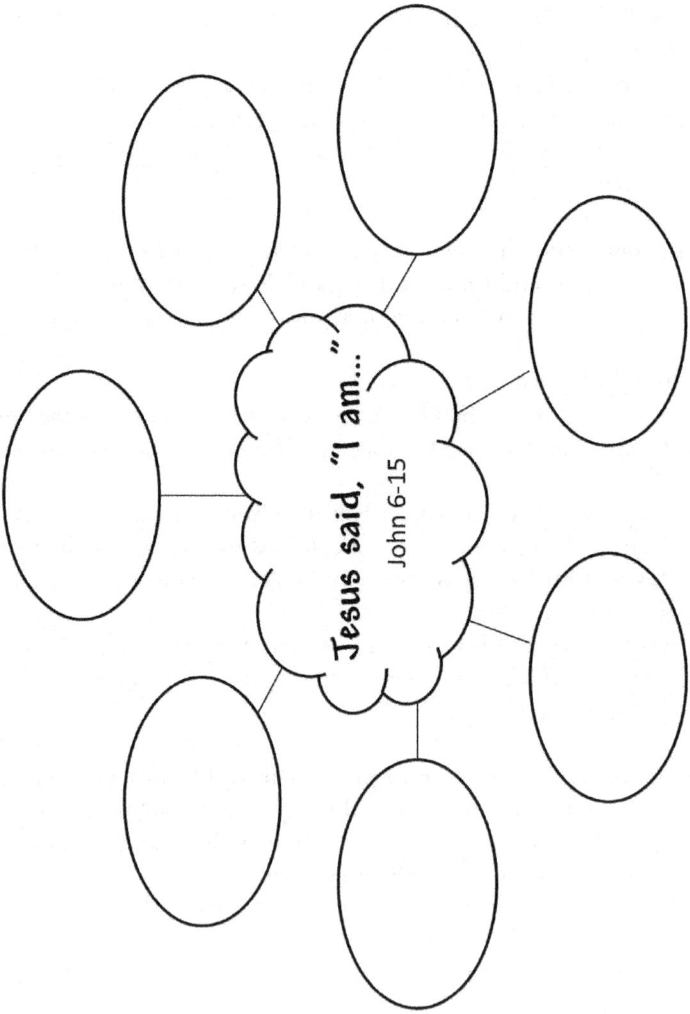

Where did the 12 tribes of Israel come from? Students fill in the lineage boxes. Most students don't realize that while Joseph was an instrumental part of God's plan of salvation, Jesus' lineage goes through Judah.

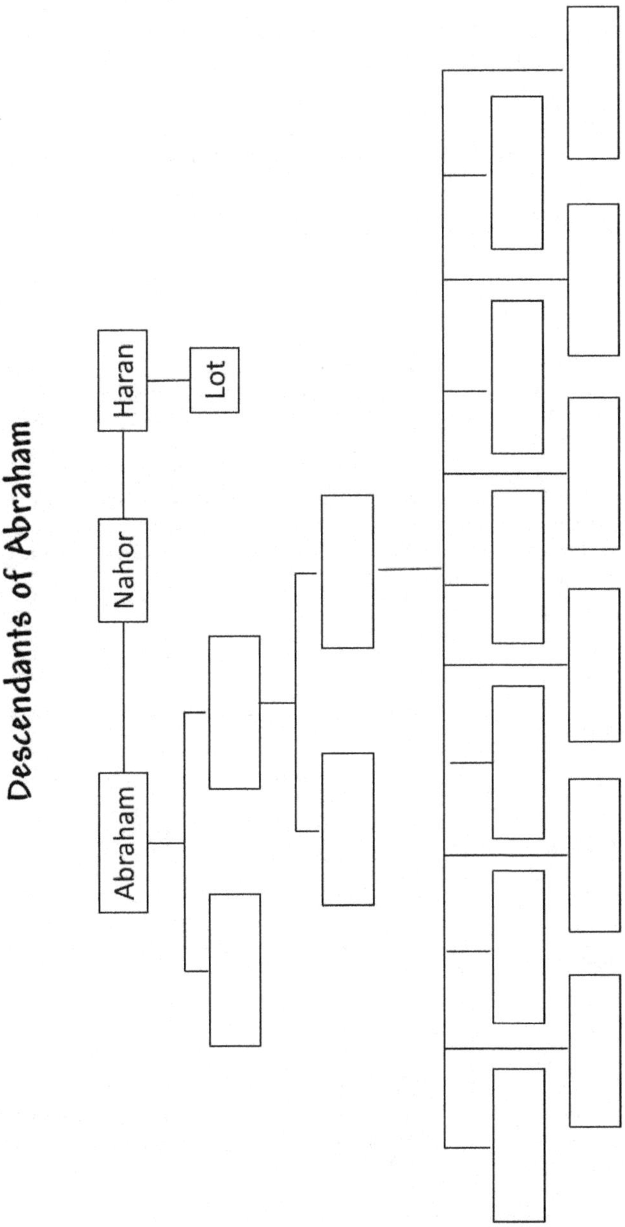

APPENDIX F
LESSON PLAN SAMPLE

The best plan is the one that works for the teacher. It contains exactly what is needed for an efficient and productive lesson. Some new teachers like more detail and experienced teachers like a bit less, but every good teacher plans their class ahead of time.

<table>
<tr><th colspan="3">CONFIRMATION LESSON PLAN</th></tr>
<tr><td colspan="2">Topic:</td><td>Date:</td></tr>
<tr><td>Goals</td><td colspan="2">List the goals for the lesson (just that day) here.</td></tr>
<tr><td>Warm-Up</td><td colspan="2">___ Pre-Quiz
___ Photo Response
___ Who Am I?
___ Take a Poll
___ Memory Check
___ Consider This…
___ Music
___ Quick Quiz
___ What does this mean?
___ Correct me if I'm Wrong…
___ Coffee Cup Theology
___ Other:</td></tr>
<tr><td rowspan="5">Lesson Activities</td><td colspan="2">First Activity—In each section add the learning activity (lecture, discussion, reading, going through the textbook or worksheet answers prior to discussion, game, etc.). Include any brain breaks or transitions to the next activity. Put each learning activity in its own box to help with organization.</td></tr>
<tr><td colspan="2">Second Activity</td></tr>
<tr><td colspan="2">Third Activity</td></tr>
<tr><td colspan="2">Fourth Activity</td></tr>
<tr><td colspan="2">Fifth Activity</td></tr>
<tr><td>Cool-Down</td><td colspan="2">___ Quick Quiz
___ Take a Poll
___ Journal Entry
___ 2 Questions
___ Recap
___ Other:
___ What does this mean?
___ Correct Me If I'm Wrong…</td></tr>
</table>

APPENDIX G
TABLE OF STRATEGIES

Warm-Ups	
Pre-Quiz	A short quiz to find out what students know about the topic of the day *before* you get started.
Photo Response	A cartoon or photo displayed that has something to do with the lesson that day; have students write a response to it.
Coffee Cup Theology	Put a misused Bible verse up for students to respond to: What's wrong with this phrase, quote, or verse?
Quick Quiz	A few review questions on what was learned last week. No T/F or multiple choice questions allowed.
Correct Me If I'm Wrong	Two truths and a lie regarding the topic to be discussed in class that day or about last week's topic for students to determine which are true and which is the lie.
Take a Poll	Poll students about something they're going to learn that day to see if they lean toward a Biblical or world teaching of it. Collect the responses and check them out at a break and/or bring them up at the end of class to see if opinions have changed.
Memory Check	Students write down the memory work for the week. Have them hand the papers in so you can see how they're doing. You can also have them write down memory work from a few weeks or a month ago as well.
What does this mean?	Have students define a couple of terms. Don't choose so many that they can't be done in about five minutes. I suggest no more than three.
Consider This	Write up a scenario similar to what somebody in the Bible faced, but make it fit students' lives today.
Who am I?	Clues that describe a prophet, Bible character, or well-known person in Church history to see if students can figure out who it is based on the clues. If they can't before time is up, give them a few more obvious clues.
Music	Have hymn or contemporary song lyrics copied for students to pick up as they arrive and ask them a few questions about it.

Learning Strategies	
Lecture Outline	Middle school attention span is 10-12 minutes. Pictures are worth a thousand words. Provide lecture outlines for students to take notes.
Graphic Organizer	Helps students organize timelines, characteristics, family trees, plots of stories, etc.
Discussion	Write discussion prompts or questions ahead of time and be prepared with strategies to get them talking. Provide discussion outlines for students to take notes.
Verbal Charades	Students pull terms out of a bowl, bucket, or hat and describe them in a way that allows other students to guess what they are to earn points. Good activity to review terms.
Ethical Dilemmas	Let students struggle with giving appropriate advice. If you have a problem coming up with dilemmas, watch popular television for examples of teenagers making poor choices.
Debate	Have students support opposite sides of the same issue. Prep students beforehand so they know what's expected.
Maps	Have blank maps for students to complete. Have them draw the journey and label interesting occurrences that happened along the way. If color coding is needed, have colored pencils available.
Questions	Ask questions in a game show fashion. Another option is to use an online game template for Jeopardy or other common television games.
Reflection Journal	Give students time to respond to a specific and thoughtful question regarding what was learned in class that day. Best done at the end of class.
Cool-Downs	
Quick Quiz	A few higher level (thinking or opinion) review questions on what was talked about that day.
Take a Poll	Poll students about something they learned that day to see if their opinions have changed based on the discussion. Collect the responses and check them out.
What does this mean?	Define a couple (no more than 3) of terms learned that day. Don't choose so many that they can't be done in about five minutes.

Questions	Students write down two questions about the topic discussed before they leave.
Recap	Share one thing that was talked about today that you didn't know before today and one thing you'd like to know more about.
Reflection Journal Entry	Have students respond to a journal question. Be sure the question gets them to think and that you see their response as they walk out the door.
The 5 W's	Before students leave, have them complete the 5 W's about what was studied that day: Who, What, When, Where, and Why.
Brain Break	
Bible Culture Corner	Give students some quick cultural information. If you need a resource, try the *Complete Bible Discovery Guide* (Concordia Publishing House).
Cartoon	Show students a funny historical cartoon you can find online. It can be used as a way to signal the end of slides or notes.
Memory Challenge	Pause for a quick memory challenge at an appropriate time or as a transition.

REFERENCES

American Psychological Association. (2002). *Developing Adolescents: A Reference for Professionals.* Washington, DC: American Psychological Association.

Barrett, J. B., Pearson, J., Muller, C., & Frank, K.A. (2007). Adolescent Religiosity and School Contexts. *Social Science Quarterly*, *88*(4), 1024-1037.

Biehler, R. F., & Snowman, J. (1982). Psychology applied to teaching (4th ed.). Boston, MA: Houghton Mifflin Co.

Burreson, K. (2009). What is Confirmation? Shaping a Word-Filled, Sacramental Life. In M. Sengele (Ed.), *Confirmation Basics* (pp. 23-32). St. Louis, MO: Concordia Publishing House.

Clark, D. R. (2004). *The Art and Science of Leadership.* Retrieved June 8, 2012 from http://nwlink.com/~donclark/leader/leader.html

Clark, D. R. (2004). *Visual, auditory, and kinesthetic learning styles (VAK).* Retrieved June 8, 2012 from http://www.nwlink.com/~donclark/hrd/styles/vakt.html

Clark, I. (2011). Formative assessment: Policy, perspective, and practice. *Florida Journal of Educational Administration and Policy, 4* (2), 158-180.

Collver, Albert (2011). *Witness Mercy Life Together Bible Study.* St. Louis, MO: Concordia Publishing House

Cripps, K. & Zyromski, B. (2009). Adolescents' psychological well-being and perceived parental involvement: Implications for parental involvement in middle schools. *Research in Middle Level Education Online, 33*(4).

Dinsmore, T. S. (2003). Classroom Management. [Unpublished paper].

Elmore, Tim (2012). Artificial Maturity: Helping kids meet the challenge of becoming authentic adults. San Francisco, CA: Jossey-Bass. p. 38

Enerson, D. M., Plank, K. M., & Johnson, R. N. (2004). Planning a class session: A guide for new teachers. University Park, PA: Schreyer Institute for Teaching Excellence.

Englehart, J. M. (2012). Five half-truths about classroom management. *The Clearing House: A Journal of Educational Strategies, Issues and Ideas, 85*(2), 70-73. doi: 10.1080/00098655.2011.616919

Holder, D. W., Durant, R. H., Harris, T. L., Daniel, J. H., Obeidallah, D., & Goodman, E. (2000). The association between adolescent spirituality and voluntary sexual activity [Abstract]. *Journal of Adolescent Health, 26*, 295-302.

Krathwohl, David R. (2002). A revision of Bloom's taxonomy: An overview. *Theory into Practice, 42*(4), 212-218.

Luther, Martin (1986) *Luther's Small Catechism with Explanation.* St. Louis, MO: Concordia Publishing House.

Luther, Martin (1525). Treatise to the councilmen of all cities in Germany. Retrieved June 7, 2012 from http://www.godrules.net/library/luther/NEW1luther_d9.htm

Lutheran Service Book (2006). St. Louis, MO: Concordia Publishing House.

Maday, T. (2008). Stuck in the middle: Strategies to engage middle-level learners. Washington, DC: The Center for Comprehensive School Reform and Improvement.

McFarland, K. P. (2000). Specific Classroom Management Strategies for the Middle/Secondary Education Classroom. [Unpublished paper].

Medina, John (2008). *Brain rules: 12 principles for surviving and thriving at work, home, and school.* Seattle, WA: Pear Press.

Medina, John (2008). Retrieved on June 2, 2014 from http://www.brainrules.net/vision?scene=

Morgan, N., & Saxton, J. (1994). Asking better questions: Models, techniques and classroom activities for engaging students in learning. Markham, Ontario: Pembroke Publishers.

No Child Left Behind (2005). *Helping your child through early adolescence.* Washington, DC: U.S. Department of Education.

Obenchain, K. M., & Taylor, S. S. (2005). Behavior management: Making it work in middle and secondary schools. *The Clearing House, 79*(1), 7-11.

Ozorak, E. W. (1989). Social and cognitive influences on the development of religious beliefs and commitment in adolescence. *Journal for the Scientific Study of Religion, 28*, 448-463.

Regnerus, M. D., Smith, C., & Smith, B. (2004). Social Context in the development of adolescent religiosity. *Applied Developmental Science,* 8(1), 27-38.

Resnick, M. D., Bearman, P. S., Blum, R. W., Bauman, K. E., Harris, K. M., Jones, J., Tabor, J., Beuhring, T., Sieving, R. E., Shew, M., Ireland, M., Bearinger, L. H., & Udry, J. R. (1997). Protecting Adolescents from harm: Findings from the National Longitudinal Study on Adolescent Health. *Journal of the American Medical Association, 278,* 823-832.

Ritchie, Anne Thackeray (1885). *Mrs. Dymond.* Great Britain: Smith, Elder, and Co.

Roberts, D. (2000). Media and youth: Access, exposure, and privatization. *Journal of Adolescent Health, 27* (supplement), 8-14.

Schurr, S. L. (1995). Prescriptions for success in heterogeneous classrooms. Columbus, OH: National Middle School Association.

Smith, T. E. (1997). Adolescent gender differences in time alone and time devoted to conversation. *Adolescence, 26*, 83-87.

Van Voorhis, F. L. (2011). Costs and benefits of family involvement in homework. *Journal of Advanced Academics, 22* (2), 220-249.

Vawter, D. (2010, January). Mining the middle school mind. *The Education Digest,* 47-49.

Wiggins, G., & McTighe, J. (2005). Understanding by design (2nd ed.). Alexandria, VA: Association for Supervision of Curriculum Development.

TOPICAL INDEX

ABOUT THE AUTHOR

Laura Langhoff is the woman behind the Carpenter's Ministry Toolbox, a Christian education resource ministry whose goal is to apply current educational research and strategies to congregational education. She dreams of equipping and encouraging pastors, other professional church workers, and volunteers to effectively educate God's children from preschool through adult. Laura is a professional educator with an M.A. in classroom instruction, administrative leadership experience, as well as Director of Christian Education (DCE) certification in the LCMS.

One of her many passions is to visit with both professional and volunteer church educators in person through workshops providing educational resources, support, and encouragement. Laura lives in Minneapolis, MN and enjoys painting watercolors and riding her bike around the lakes.

More free resources are available at www.dceministry.blogspot.com

Bible Reading Plans with guides for middle and high school students are available at www.carpentersministrytoolbox.com

65126255R00050

Made in the USA
Middletown, DE
01 September 2019